Tennessee Claflin Cook

Constitutional Equality

A Right of Woman

Tennessee Claflin Cook

Constitutional Equality
A Right of Woman

ISBN/EAN: 9783337365776

Printed in Europe, USA, Canada, Australia, Japan

Cover: Foto ©Suzi / pixelio.de

More available books at **www.hansebooks.com**

CONSTITUTIONAL EQUALITY

A RIGHT OF WOMAN;

—OR—

A CONSIDERATION OF THE VARIOUS RELATIONS WHICH
SHE SUSTAINS AS A NECESSARY PART OF THE

BODY OF SOCIETY AND HUMANITY;

With Her Duties to Herself—together with a Review of the

CONSTITUTION OF THE UNITED STATES,

SHOWING THAT THE RIGHT TO VOTE IS GUARANTEED TO
ALL CITIZENS.

ALSO A REVIEW OF THE RIGHTS OF CHILDREN.

By TENNIE C. CLAFLIN.

NEW YORK:
WOODHULL, CLAFLIN & CO., 44 BROAD STREET.
1871.

INTRODUCTORY.

The importance which the movement for equal political and civil rights, without regard to sex, is assuming, makes it incumbent upon those who have made the subject a study to spread before the inquiring public such phases of their experi. ence and deductions as will tend to promote accurate thought upon the subject. It does not do in these times to stifle a new evolution of civilization by treating it with contempt. There are too many intelligent, unbiased minds now existing to allow this step to be utterly ignored, as has been proposed by those who oppose it. It will be obvious to the careful reader that the series of papers which are now offered have been prepared with the view of gradually leading the mind to acknowledge that women are something more than " things;" that they are thinking, reasoning, even accountable beings, and as capable of self-government as most men are. We feel that we are in duty bound to advocate the perfect equality of all human beings, which may, without assumption, be called the cause of humanity. We know there is a great amount of prejudice against women voting, in both sexes; but we also know that it is simply prejudice—the same prejudice which all new developments of thought and science are always met by—and that it only requires to be met by a persistent presentation of the realities of the question to in time divest the people of it.

Our purpose in the construction of this book, in the beginning, development and ending, will be apparent to all who peruse it entire, and we make no apology for any seeming inconsistencies or seeming change of argument. But this we will say: The basis of all true humanitarian reform—or rather growth—lies in the "coming generation." With the present little can be done; with the future everything.

We request a thorough examination, and afterward a rigid though just judgment; and thus we commit our work to the care of the public, with whom " the right always comes uppermost" in the end.

TENNIE C. CLAFLIN.

New York, February 1, 1871.

CONTENTS.

CONTENTS.

EQUALITY FOR WOMAN.

There seems to have been from time immemorial connected with the word "Woman," a certain sense of servitude. Woman has always been considered something less than "Man" in many distinguishing respects. Even in infancy, before the light of intelligence sparkles in the eye, the daughter is mourned over by the fond mother, because she is not a son who may rise to honor and fame, and live long ages in the memory of the world.

The facts of history, personal observation, and sad experience, perhaps, compel the mother to feel that, for her child, lying in innocent helplessness upon her breast, there is no hope in the future, other than the common fate of woman, unless, perchance, God may have bestowed upon her the germ of extraordinary beauty. With this thought startling her soul, her prayers ascend to heaven that her infant may be so endowed, and that thus, in after years, she may find favor in the eyes of some one high in authority, riches or position, and may be able to compensate him with her beauty, who should condescend to woo her. Beauty has risen from the cot to the palace; from the shepherdess to the queen. It is not to be wondered, then, that mothers pray for the bestowal of this gift in which lies their daughter's only hope; although they remember that its possession, rich as it is in itself, appeals directly to that portion of man's nature which, finding expression through such appeals, has left a blight upon the very name of woman, when beauty has fled from her.

It is not desired to weave around the condition of woman a veil that shall hide her true worth and nobility, nor to convey the idea that beauty, or its lacking, is the sole determining power of her destiny; but

2 EQUALITY FOR WOMAN.

it is desirable that what there is of disgrace and misfortune in her condition should be kept up to the enlightened gaze of mankind and receive its verdict of disapproval.

In the tender years of childhood, and the more important ones of
youth, a variety of influences govern the growth of the body and the
development of the mind. The boy is educated with some distinct personal point to be gained. He is taught that if he *will*, he *may*, that he
has but to make the requisite effort, and success will surely crown him.
With the stimulus of future attainment constantly poured upon the
growing youth, by those to whom he looks for nothing but good coun-
sel and advice, is it to be wondered that so many born even in obscurity
and extreme poverty, have become brilliant lights in the world of science, literature and government?

As the youth approaches manhood, he is pressed into some special
channel of thought and culture, for which his mind and talent seem to
be inclined, and all the aid, material and intellectual, it is possible to
furnish, is extended to assist and encourage. Thus strengthened and
accoutered, he prepares to commence life for himself.

How different is it with the girl!

Is it instilled into her mind, morning, noon and night, that, by
stern trial and application in any particular direction, she may attain to
eminence before the world, and fill a niche in its temple of honor and
fame? Is she taught to apply herself to philosophy, that by an understanding of its already known laws and principles she may discover some
new light? Is it to astronomy her attention is called, that in deep research and calculation some new world may be added to our present
known systems; or some law discovered that shall explain motions and
influences not yet accounted for? Is she taught to dive into the bowels
of the earth and bring up new treasures with which to break away the
shackles of superstition, ignorance or fear, and, by chemical analysis
thereof, unveil some of the hidden mysteries of association whereby so
very few elementary principles produce so great variety and diversity as
all nature, animate and inanimate, presents to the delighted eye and the
wondering mind? Is her intuitive mind and brain directed to natural
philosophy to discover new modes of applying or generating power,
whereby the muscular world shall be relieved from some of its burdens
of labor and fatigue, and the mind given time for growth and expan-
sion? Are the intricate workings of the mind held up for her solution?
Does she seek for the laws that direct and govern the association and in-
terchange of unspoken thought? Is she asked, Whence cometh that

new thought, never before expressed—that new idea, never before presented? Is her attention attracted to the study of the laws of nations and of society, that from their defects something new and better may spring? Is her mind ever directed to these channels, with the suggestion that she must some day, and that not far distant, be prepared to assist in the halls of Legislation, state and national, to frame and propose laws better adapted to the growing condition of mankind than those now existing?

Is the fact that begins to stand so prominently before the eyes of this country, that woman must become associated in the administration of its laws, presented to her growing mind, and she encouraged to become fitted therefor? Aye, and more. Is it ever hinted to her that the woman may even now be who shall fill that highest office in the gift of the people?

In the name of the demand now going up for female suffrage, have any preparatory incentives been held before the growing girl, the blushing maiden, the budding woman? In vain may we listen for any general affirmation, and scarcely may we expect any special exceptional cases; and if, perchance, there are, it will be found, upon close analysis, they are the result of inspirational, rather than educational, causes.

The parents of the present generation can but hang their heads in shame, and confess that they have seen no beacon-light in the future for their daughters for which they should trim their sails and set their rudders, with a stern determination that, come storm or raging sea, it shall be reached; on the contrary, what have they done? this and nothing more: they have taught the coming generation, as all past ones have been taught, that, in the duties of the wife and the cares of the mother the destiny of woman is attained; and, adhering to the principles of Paul, insist that, to reach beyond those well-defined boundaries, is indelicate and unfeminine in the extreme.

To be accomplished is of much greater importance, in the general estimation, than to be useful; to ape the past a much more ready way to become accomplished than to delve into the present and future; to commit the sayings and doings of others to memory, a much better and easier way to prepare to show themselves well-bred, well-read, and well-disciplined for all occasions, than to search out and stand true and firm upon principles, and to rely implicitly upon deductions therefrom for support and guidance; to shine by personal ornamentation and borrowed light, is held in higher esteem than a polished interior, lighted by clear intuition and uncompromising reason.

How common is the remark that all educated women write alike! Pursue the inquiry a little further and deeper, and see if they do not closely resemble each other in very many things. Little else can be expected. Are they not all educated to the same point—trained for the same purpose? Overlooking or ignoring all the natural capacities and inclinations of the mind, they are and have been trained specially for the matrimonial market, and it can be called nothing else. Nor has their training looked to any point beyond the mere fact of marriage—just as though in that point existence ceased. How many know aught of the duties, cares, responsibilities, trials, sufferings, that fall to her after reaching what should really be considered the beginning of her actual, individual life? A general answer rises from woman, Few, very few! Still less is the number wise enough in themselves to find in all those seeming sources of sorrow the never-exhaustible fountain of joy and happiness, which the Great Creator has ordained shall flow to all who enter its sacred portals with wisdom, understanding, and love sufficient to make the life currents of two, flow in and through the same channels of peace and harmony.

No relation on earth so sacred as that of husband and wife. Round it gathers a halo of light and divinity before whose potent power the lowest of human beings falls down and worships, and from whose holy purity the basest shrinks in shame.

In the potent charm that attends the association of man and woman is found the strongest argument for her emancipation. It is a power needed everwhere, and the world cannot much longer afford to deprive itself of its benefits. It is argued by the superficial thinker of either sex, that if woman enters the busy outer world and mingles with its scenes, she must necessarily lose that peculiar charm and characteristic that now everywhere commands the respect and admiration of man. This is a conclusion arrived at without evidence, reason or argument, and will not stand the test of either.

Is a woman less a woman because she stands before an audience and holds it spell-bound by her eloquence and logic? Because she argues for her client in the halls of justice? Because she maintains her propositions in legislative and congressional assemblies? Because she assists in executing the country's laws? Because she is president of a bank, a railroad? Because she invents some labor-saving machine? Because she alleviates the distressed invalid? In short, is a woman any less a woman because she aspires to and performs any of the duties which the Creator has given her faculties to perform, and which justice, honor and a noble ambition inspire every well-born soul to accomplish for humanity?

Anything less than an utter repudiation of the prejudices, the ignorance of the past, is unworthy the enlightened sense and reason of this century. May we not, before its close, expect to see such absurd libels upon the name of woman and the consistency of man blotted from the hearts and minds of mankind, and expect to see woman welcomed to any and all spheres of life and action for which, by nature or inclination, she is fitted?

Henceforth let it go broadcast to the world—from every woman's lips, at least—that the more she accomplishes by her own exertions in any direction or honorable calling, the more a woman she is; and, instead of detracting from her native graces, this shall add to the beauty and lustre of all her perfections, making her more to be admired by all.

Nor need it be feared that contact with the busy world will result disastrously to woman's general standard of purity and morals. On the contrary, very much benefit may reasonably be expected from the union of her influence with that of man in every department of life and activity. Very few of man's imperfections and vices find expression within the bosom of his home circle and its connections. Suppose home influences are extended everywhere. Will they not produce the same saving, healthful effects upon action and thought without deteriorating the fountain whence they flow?

How long would drinking-saloons, gambling-hells, houses of prostitution exist, did the wife and sister go hand in hand with the husband and brother in the various pursuits of life, aiding in all their endeavors and cheering their every effort, and, by so doing, make their interests mutual, their wishes one and their privileges equal?

Nothing can be more fallacious and unfortunate than the proposition that man is entitled to special immunities in transgressing the laws of purity, honor and virtue. Man and woman alike should be amenable to the same judgment of society and law. Man should be held to the same moral law that is now imposed on woman, and the latter should enjoy the same choice of action and occupation that is now accorded to the former. The claim for equality does not imply that she shall wildly and recklessly rush from her present paths into the ways of dissipation and vice which man frequents. It is not an equality of degredation and disgrace that is sought, but one of the noblest developments of her powers and faculties.

Let it be asked, Where lies the cause of the condition in which all inharmonies between the sexes arise, and where the solution, the remedy? Can it be sought out and overcome by direct legislation? Years of fruitless attempts have demonstrated the futility of this, even as a palliative. Will the right of suffrage extended to woman produce the desired result? Scarcely; although this would undoubtedly be a step in the right direction, and, as such, a mitigation, in so far as it lessens the distance between the respective standpoints of man and woman. While, then, you are asking earnestly for this extension, do not forget that far behind its withholding lie the roots of what you wish destroyed.

Were your vision outraged by an unsightly, poisonous tree, you would not attempt its destruction by first lopping off a few of its longest branches, and thus work from the circumference inward, but you would lay your axe to its very roots, and, by one grand felling, destroy it forever. Where, then, are the roots of the pernicious tree that has grown to such dimensions and extended its branches in such alarming directions?

How shall what is desired be reduced to a proposition so simple and plain that all may understand it? Is it not that there shall be perfect equality to man and woman in all things, wherein equality can, by nature, exist? Man is educated toward this point; woman away from it. In woman, then, lies the cause, and in her must be found its solution, and she must apply the remedy.

It cannot be denied that both sexes are born equal, possessed of the same essential germinal qualities of character, conscience and intellect, and entitled to the same blessing of growth and development, the reception of which would conduce to their continual equality. The point of divergence between the sexes, then, commences just were similarity of education leaves off, where self-reliance is taught the male, and future dependence the female. The legitimate consequence of this teaching is "servitude." Woman must be grown and educated with the idea of equality always before her, and not the fact that, at some future time, she is to surrender herself into the keeping of a husband, upon whom forever after she is to be dependent. The past records of this condition stand full of sorrow before us, stained all over by the tears of the broken-hearted wife, mother and sister, and call loudly and earnestly that they never again be reproduced. Be sure, then, mothers and daughters, that you be prepared to demand and receive, measure for measure, what is asked of you and granted. Become self-reliant and self-supporting. How many women are to-day adding to the wealth of the world by productive labor, or are even self-support-ing? How many fortunes are squandered in the vain attempt to make up by external show what is lacking in interior wealth?

Thank God! the time is rapidly approaching, and even now is, in which woman begins to be valued and appreciated for the amount of brains she can command, rather than the extent of show she can make. This standard already holds with men, but it is to be regretted that women of intellect are still regarded by so many of their own sex with a feeling bordering upon disdain.

Equal rights call upon women to look upon the sacred relations of marriage as of joint and perfect equality in all respects, and at the same time *so mutual* that all individual interest and desires become one in aim, purpose and pursuit; anything short of this, no matter with how much solemnity husband and wife may have been pronounced, is no *perfect* marriage in the sight of Heaven.

A question asked is often productive of as much good as a propo-sition demonstrated; then let it be asked: What would be the condi-tion and relations of men and women twenty-five years hence, could it be possible that to-morrow an edict should go forth, sufficiently potent and general, demanding that henceforth the education and incentives of the sexes should be the same, according to the natural faculties and not accord-ing to arbitrary rule; that the same responsibilities and duties would be imposed upon them, and it should be theirs to accept and perform them without the possibility of a doubt? Do you think at the end of that time conventions would have to be held to organize efforts, asking legis-lation about your rights? Rather do you not know that the fact of your having prepared yourselves to incur and exercise those rights, would appeal to existing laws of nations and customs of society, with a power nothing could resist, and if resisted, the obstacles would be swept away as by the hurricane?

In conclusion, let us remember that while the various unphilo-sophic, unfortunate and incongruous conditions of women are receiving separate and divided attention from separate and divided efforts, these, good and acceptable as they are in themselves, may fail to do all that is expected of them. At the same time let it be remembered that re-forms, based upon principles and ideas, and which deal with causes, though their seeming progress may be slow, are as certain as the com-ing sun's rising, or the ebb and flow of old ocean's mighty tidal breathings.

WOMAN'S POSITION.

HER NECESSITIES AND HER NEEDS.—THE REASONABLENESS OF THEM—
EXTENSION OF THESE NECESSARY TO INDUCE PREPARATION.

It cannot be denied that the position of woman in all practical matters is inferior to man. While she at present is incapable of maintaining such an equality, she excels in other respects; but these are chiefly such as do not add to personal fame or real importance. However much distinction there may be in the natural characteristics of the sexes, the time is now come when woman shall enter an enlarged sphere of action and use.

In making the innovation upon customs which the present condition contemplates, it is of essential importance that the boundaries of nature be not overstepped. Every advance made, should have the sanction of adaptetion and use. When brute force was the ruling power—when vast armies decided the rights of kings—woman was but of little importance. The general influence woman is now capable of exerting is immense, and it will be used either for good or ill; by being diverted into unfortunate channels, it becomes a source of sorrow and misery, but when properly directed no power is more healthful and productive of good. Could all the noble qualities of the sex be well directed, the world's progress would be vastly accelerated.

If we admit the present condition of woman as unfortunate, and that this arises from her being man's practical inferior, she must then become his equal by the same means he became what he is. She must be educated to serve the same general purpose. She is not possessed of the qualities necessary to face breastworks bristling with bayonets, and from which the screaming shell and rattling grape pour unmercifully forth. The means of conquest being modified, woman's talent is required to meet the new demands arising from the situation; besides, it is necessary to open channels for the expenditure of her growing power.

Instead of the prevalent idea that in the duties of the wife, the individuality of the woman must be lost, there must obtain the wider view, that when she becomes the wife, the truer and better part of her mission begins. Instead of that condition being the chief end to be attained, it must be regarded as but one of the incidents of life which leads to wider fields of usefulness. Marriage does not interfere with the general duties of man. He is not educated with the idea before him, that he is preparing to be the husband; from childhood the thought of independence is the main one; he strives to become fitted for some special sphere of action to which his inclinations tend. Let woman pursue the same course; let her learn to be independent; self reliant; self supporting; then she will never be thrown upon the mercy of the world nor driven to conditions against which her soul revolts.

With such changes in the preparation of woman for the active du- ties of life, the greater one now demanded will come. Though woman can never be like man, she can be his equal in all the rights and privi- leges of life.

Among these privileges, none seems more just than that of having a voice in choosing those ; who shall make the laws to which she in com- mon with man must be subject. Reverse the situation: would man quietly submit as woman has, and does? Should he then deny to wo- man this privilege? It is no argument that the majority of women do not desire suffrage. If but one in a thousand does, she should not be restrained from it, upon any plea of indifference on the part of the 999.

Suffrage alone cannot elevate woman. It will prove, however, an in- centive for her to attain wider experience. Ambition is as common in woman as in man; if her sphere of action is enlarged her realm of pos- sibilities will be proportionately extended. In this sense, and for this reason, suffrage is desirable. It will open a new avenue for thought and action ; it will tend to draw attention from the frivolities of fashion and society, and in many instances to protect her from the debasing allure- ments of immorality and vice. With new incentives offered, change in education would come. Accomplishment, simply as such, would be dis- carded and practical life anticipated.

Woman will not prepare for responsibilities, or duties she is de- barred from entering upon. She will not educate to practice law, while she is denied admission to the bar. But if this and other spheres are opened, she will prepare to enter them and compete for the prizes they offer.

Let man acknowledge that woman has the right to become his equal by removing all barriers, so that the charge of domination may no longer be used against him. Let there be an opportunity for practical equality, so that equal justice can obtain. Let there be practical freedom so that limited equality may cease to exist.

THE FUTURE OF AMERICAN WOMEN.

THE WITHHOLDING OF PRIVILEGE THE CAUSE OF UNDEVELOPMENT
—THE DUTIES OF MOTHERS—WOMAN'S INTEREST IN GOVERNMENT
EQUAL TO MAN'S—MOMENTOUS EVENTS ABOUT TO TRANSPIRE.

In the past there has been little to stimulate women to the acquisition of practical knowledge. They have thought of little else
than trying to be most attractive to the eye of man. They give no
consideration to the possibility of ever being called to step from the
common routine of a wife's life; even for this they have been badly
prepared. In short, the idea has been "the conquest" that should
"make their market," without any understanding of the duties involved.

True, the avenues to distinction have mostly been closed against
them. They have never been encouraged to break the barriers down,
to obtain an *entree* to the race being run beyond, by their brothers, who
have guarded their "special rights" and privileges with such jealous
care that they have shut out all knowledge of them.

Whenever a brave soul has attempted innovations upon these
rights and privileges, the anathemas of both sexes have been hurled
indiscriminately at her. Persuasion first, anything next, is used, to
force her to retire to the needle and the kitchen. Perhaps, stung by
defeat and driven by bitter experience to think all the world a mock-
ery, she flies to the only seeming escape from herself—to the brutality
of her pursuer, and becomes thereby the proscribed of society, while he
remains its ornament. And this is the equality guaranteed to woman.

This has been: it remains to be determined what shall be, though
what is, is ominous of it. Revolutions based upon principles of right
never go backward. If they be resisted by conservative indifference

or pharisaical godliness, the spirit which compels them will the more certainly destroy the obstacles and their raisers. The demand has been made by woman for equality, in the matter, duties and privileges of life. It will never be recalled until they are fully accorded. The more and longer those who have them at their command say "No!" the severer will be their reckoning. Gentlemen, yield gracefully while you may. If delayed until you must, it will not be graciously received.

The signs of the times are full of meaning. Mothers, are you awake to their portentions? Have you no stern duty to perform in view of them? You know from bitter experience much which your daughters have not even dreamed of, or at most, have seen from such an enchanting distance, that the deformities have appeared beautiful. You have learned woman's lesson of life. You have not taught your daughters what you have learned. You will still compel them to acquire by experience what you could have taught them. Society is hollow, false and untrue, but you did not learn it at the "boarding school" where you "finished your education," Heaven save the mark! You were not taught independent self-reliance, but that it was a shame to soil your delicate hands by labor. When death or other cause has taken your reliance, what has your finished education done toward maintaining your family? To do this you have been driven to all manner of expedients—to hasty and detestable unions and often to revolting necessities—simply because you were not properly educated. By the wisdom acquired through your experience let your daughters profit. Let them not be able in after life to remember you as having failed in any single duty, they will or may learn you could have performed. Let not one experience, however disagreeable, escape them, for that very one may prove the rock of their salvation.

It is time for woman to become earnest, practical—competent to pursue the journey of life alone, if need be, to maintain an equality with men wherever the order of nature permits, and to cease to be frivolously accomplished for the drawing-room, the ball-room and society, and especially is it time to cease to be man's mere appendage.

Many men may choose the weak, yielding woman, with no positive individuality. If they do, it is because their practices are such as their equals would not endure. Man may affect perfect simplicity in women, but when they fall within the sphere of intellect and capacity, exhibited with earnestness and purity, they will worship there, and so long as he remains within the reach of this influence, "duties" are lost sight of.

If all women receive similar advantages in education, there will still be grades of attainment. Nature, in all her operations, presents gradations. Woman is an object of it; so is man. Similar grades gravitate toward each other. The lower may admire the higher, but under this law cannot attain it. This series of grades constitutes the fabric of society.

The end to be attained by education, is, to fit individuals to fill the various positions in society. Education, in the strictest sense, is life-long. We use it relatively and as applying to the rudimentary part of life, and in inviting the attention of mothers to the immediate future, we ask them, if their duties will have been performed, in view of it, if they make no modifications in the preparation of their daughters to meet it? Suffrage will be extended to woman, and will open the way to various fields of industry for her, and will give her equality therein. Woman has as much at stake in government as man, and should feel as great interest in its proper administration. To do this she must understand its principles. How many of the mothers of the countries understand the processes and forms of government, or the policies that underlie it; or can explain the difference between a tariff for revenue and protection, between *ad valorem* and specific duties and the policies that indicate them, or can tell the significance of "moving the previous question," or rising to a "privileged question," or to a "point of order?"

It is to such and other practical directions, in which you have never even looked, that the attention of your daughters should be called. They should be taught that they will be obliged to participate, in all branches of the public service which are now conducted solely by men. They should be ambitious to be well prepared to accept and perform these duties well. Music, French and drawing are excellent in their places, but they will scarcely help you maintain political equality, and thus it is with the greater part of female education.

Social conditions are volcanic, and are so pregnant with danger, that none may tell what the situation a dozen months hence may be. It behooves woman to be prepared for whatever may come, so that, if deprived of support from one source, she may not be forced to obnoxious means to obtain it from another. As soon as your daughters attain sufficient age and experience, put them to practical tasks, as you do your sons. They are as capable of assuming responsibilities and performing regular duties as your sons are. They should be made to regard labor as honorable, never as disgraceful. They should be taught that every morsel of food, every article of raiment and every expense incurred, which depend upon the price of another's labor, is dishonestly appropriated, for the "workmen is worthy of his hire." If he be willing to part with his "hire," to supply the demands of your ignorance, stupidity or indolence, it is none the less shameful of you to accept it, and still more so, to be obliged to do so. Momentous political, moral, religious and social problems are about to be solved. Be warned, mothers and daughters, so that they come not upon you and find your lights dim and your lamps untrimmed. Be not called upon to perform a single duty, and find yourselves unprepared to assume it, and thereby disprove your right to the equality you seek.

WOMAN AS A SOCIAL ELEMENT.

ARE WOMEN A PART OF SOCIETY?—HAVE THEY ANY RIGHTS?—WHO
SHALL DEFINE THEM?—THE CONDITION OF SOCIETY BEHIND RE-
SPECTABILITY—THE DIFFERENCE.

The larger portion of the human family is female; the disparity
comes from death in battle and from casualties, arising from man's peculiar employment, rather than from difference in numbers born.
Society is male and female. The science of society—sociology—teaches
the relations that should exist between them, and the special sphere of
each in them. One of the legitimate, because natural, results of these
relations, is offspring; these, it is woman's mission to bear, as it is so
determined by the order of nature, everywhere. The ultimate earthly
end attained by the creation—evolution—of man, was the elimination
of spirit—life—from matter; the individualization of souls, from the
homogenious mass of life existing in the material universe. Whatever
other parts the human family play in earth life, the one of reproduction
is that upon which they hinge. But is this all that is allotted to man
and woman to perform? Do their duties begin and end in the purely
domestic?

From childhood, unless compelled by the pecuniary circumstances
of her parents, woman does little else than eat, drink, sleep and flirt,
and prepare for the marriage market.• So far as practical utility is concerned, she is a mere cipher in value to society. Married, she assumes
the onerous (?) duties of the household; and thus one half the human
family are born, live and die, reaching nothing beyond this.

Allowing that, on an average, five years of woman's life are necessarily withdrawn from all other duties by those of maternity, what
becomes of the remainder? Are the remaining thirty to be spent in

nothingness because these five must be so devoted? Suppose for the moment there was no such institution as marriage, and that the world was replenished by other means, would the life of man be materially different from what it is? Would he cease his money getting, his business vocations? Would there be fewer cities built, less grand progress made? Scarcely. Man, then, is the positive element in society, while woman idles her time away in vain nothings, living merely as his appendage, to minister to his caprices and passions, and when she cannot prevent, to bear him children. It is but little to say, she has charge of the home; the duties are all performed by servants, and would proceed as regularly, were she engaged in some other duties, as she is, a large part of her time, in the pursuit of fashion. The children are in the hands of the governess or at school, and scarcely give her a thought. Her domestic duties, then, are reduced by present practice to child-bearing, and these, be it said to her shame, she is pretty effectually disposing of.

'Tis true that women can and do exert great influence over men, often swaying them into courses they would not otherwise pursue; but it will be found that this influence rarely proceeds from the wife, and is as often deleterious as beneficial. The influence of the wife, as such, forms no part of the power of society; while the influence of the woman as a member of society is powerful, and is more frequently detrimental to her as the wife and to home relations than otherwise. Man, having once felt this decided influence from woman, becomes dissatisfied, thinks any woman better than his wife, takes no pleasure in home, spends his time at his "club," or with the woman who has taught him, that some of her sex are a power in the world. In the meantime his home becomes the scene of legitimate results. The wife, finding she is no longer an attraction, that her society is distasteful, and she barely tolerated, grieves at first, next remonstrates, and then threatens: thus the breach is begun. Temptation, lying in wait for this, steps in, and she too often follows the example set her, and thus the rupture is completed, never again to be completely healed.

It is useless to attempt to blind our eyes to the present social condition; facts, too numerous and hideous, stand too prominently before us. We cannot escape them if we would, and should not if we could. Nor will it mend matters to gloss them over and label them sound, when they are only putrid. Unveil New York at midnight—or, as for time, at midday—the scenes disclosed would show our social system to be ripe for revolution, and that to defer it is to make matters worse.

It is the duty of every one to sound the alarm. Wives will no longer quietly submit to their husbands' spending time and money upon other women, nor husbands to seeing their wives decked with the "furbelows" of fashion paid for by their dishonor.

Women will not be satisfied to remain a social unit any longer. They are verging on the determination to assert equal privileges, and to share no more responsibility than men do for it. Or, if they are forever to be under the ban of society for one false step, they are determined their partners who accompany them shall be held equally culpable. Nor can man evade the point at issue. He must be willing to conform to the same rules he compels woman to do, or admit her to those he practices. The extent this condition has actually reached, without his consent, is little dreamed of by the unlearned in the ways of the times. Public prostitution is but nothing compared to that practiced under the cloak of marriage. The latter is increasing to such an extent as to threaten the existence of the former, whose representatives every year become lower and more fearfully debauched.

Deplorable as this condition is, it will only gain strength and limit by attempted concealment. It is a vile carbuncle on the body of society that requires the lancet from the hand of every one who can use it fearlessly. It cannot be absorbed again into the body; it must ripen and discharge, after which the body may become healthy. The cure, however, does not lie in this direction. Prevention is the only competent remedy, and that lies in the hands of the women, who are still the representatives of purity and self-honor, *and with them only.* Let every woman who esteems virtue and abhors prostitution in her sisters equally abhor licentiousness in her brothers. If it is disgraceful for her to associate with the woman, who has overstepped the boundary, let it be held equally so for her to associate with the man who accompanied her. (We know we are approaching forbidden ground, nevertheless we proceed.) Woman cannot do this—we speak generally—for she is dependent upon man for the means of subsistence. She has not learned to be independent, and must, therefore, condemn the woman while she tolerates the man. What is the actual distinction in the debasement of the two? Both endure it for the same reason—support. One has merited her disgrace by her willing association with the man whom the other is compelled to tolerate. Whitewashing this condition will no longer hide its black deformity. Both sides of this question must be held up—exposed to the light of reason—then let those without taint or tarnish among you cast the stones that shall designate who are the most guilty.

The scales of justice in which woman has been weighed have been fearfully against her, and in favor of man. She demands that they be balanced ; and we demand, in the name of all that is still pure and holy, that woman shall no longer shield man, by her toleration, from being weighed with her sister, and having equal judgment pronounced against him. From such an equality as must arise from such practice, and from the additonal equality that can only flow from pecuniary independence on the part of woman, can the most perfect beauty and purity in marriage be evolved. Round it will gather a halo of light and divinity, from which all baseness, impurity and license will shrink in shame, and woman will become a social element of power and importance.

WOMAN AS A POLITICAL ELEMENT.

WHAT MAINTENANCE COSTS HER—HER POWER AND INFLUENCE AS A
LOBBYIST—COULD THEY NOT BE DIRECTED IN BETTER CHANNELS?—
WOMAN THE "LEAVEN" WHICH SHALL LEAVEN THE "WHOLE LUMP"
OF HUMANITY.

Woman has been considered the negative element of the social
world. In society she has been the necessarily submissive portion. She
has had no direct means of making herself felt as a positive power in
shaping the current of events. She has been in the stream, has floated
with it, and has formed the producing part of it, but has not had the
necessary power to either modify or direct its course. She has been
allowed the opportunity of education, but the avenues for applying it
have been closed upon her. She has been permitted to stand beside
man, and to be called his "better half," while he has had the absolute
control of all she is, except the possibility of thought. For this slavery
she has been allowed the miserable compensation of support and maintenance. She has had the privilege of being possessed of property decreed to her, and at the same time denied the right to control it. She
has been obliged to contribute to the support of government, but has
been barred, not only from performing any of its functions, but from
having any voice, in any way, in its construction and administration.
She has been a political slave.

There have been exceptional instances of women rising above these
limitations; being denied the privileges they feel an inherent right to be
possessed of, they have exhibited *finesse*, when they otherwise would
have operated by direct means. Where a noble possession of talent
should have had the privilege of exhibition, a presumptive impudence
has been obliged to manifest itself, which, relying upon the consideration conscious superiority generally accords, to supposed or actual in-

feriority, approaches, insinuates and accomplishes. By such methods woman has made the power she really possesses, felt, politically, and has thereby demonstrated that she would become in a better sense than in name "man's better half," were the avenues opened to her.

It is remarked that woman will lose what present influence she possesses, by the extension of political usefulness to her. It may be answered, that this would be only true in exceptional cases, and that ninety of every hundred have no extent of influence of this kind to lose. 'Tis true that the most successful lobbyists are women; equally so that all grand pecuniary schemes, which require to be forced through legislation, seek the aid of their most accomplished representatives. If this is the species of influence she is to lose by the acquisition of political equality, and this the argument against it, it only requires to be so presented and understood to become an exploded fallacy.

Women in general know nothing of these things, and, we regret to say, are easily lulled into satisfaction by the simple presentation of arguments which have no possible application to the point their attention is to be diverted from. Woman's sphere is held up before her and painted in most vivid colors, in the consideration of which she fails to perceive that it is man who makes its limits and embellishes its area. Women are well aware that but few men are impervious to the free use of the various charms they possess; but how lamentably insulting to their dignity is it to accept this possession as an equivalent for the voluntary acquiescence in that which leaves the decision of all they may influence by it in the hands of man.

If we must judge from the position assumed by the opponents of political equality, it must be decided that it is entirely one of selfishness. The power they have they do not wish to divide. One-tenth of all available males are in one way or another connected with governmental affairs. It would be a considerable surrender of patronage to divide this with woman; besides, man has not arrived at that stage of even justice that will give to every one his due unless compelled; and most stoutly of all does he deny that political equality is due woman. By what principle of right is this denial made by those who possess the power only by sufferance? Who has ordained that man only is a political element? The truth of the matter is, that in the evolution of society, man has become possessed of a privilege to which *he knows* he has no special inherent right, but which he is not disposed to relinquish one iota of his hold upon, even to those. he professes to hold in such reverence and esteem; his objection to doing so being that he does not desire her to become contaminated by the debauchery and villainous practices it is supported by.

If the political system of yours, that you would so jealously guard woman from, is so frightfully debased and corrupted that it will defile her to touch it, it is full time its condition be thoroughly exposed. Least of all will women, who have regard for the future, remain quiet under a system of abominations that will not admit of contact without pollution. If she cannot join your caucusses, because of the roughness there exhibited, let that element be cast out. If she cannot attend the polls, without fear of violence and riot, let those who produce violence and riot be put in charge of the strong arm of government, which should, at least, be powerful enough to compel order in its most important branch.

Women will neither be violent nor riotous; must she forego any privilege because others less worthy are? It should be your first duty to guard these special privileges you possess from such fallacious arguments lest your own rights be demolished by them. What can be expected to result from a system of governing that finds root in such evil? What but subserviency to the powers that elevate can be expected from position acquired through the means of packed caucusses and fraudulent elections? Every person who is pushed into office, by the power of money, expects to double his investment during his tenure. So long as these things are so, it is presumptive folly to talk of the purity of legislation or of administration.

There is but one remedy, and that is to infuse into the body politic a new and purifying element—a leaven that shall leaven the whole. In woman this element, this leaven, can be found. Look where you will in nature, upon unequal distributions of the male and female elements, and you will find suffering resulting therefrom. Such distributions are not in accordance with the natural order of things. Creation is male and female throughout. A part of its operation, is the evolution of society. Society is male and female. Government is the most important feature of the evolution of society, but here the female element is denied admission. Woman a politician! And why not, if by so being politics can be made healthful and pure? To be a politician does not necessarily imply that one must be a knave. Nor does it follow, if woman is allowed political position, that either politics or woman will suffer degradation thereby.

Rising to the consciousness of the inferior position she has so long voluntarily occupied, woman begins to realize that she is not only passively declining privileges, but actually ignoring duties. To whatever depths of degradation some of the sex have fallen, woman, as a whole, is possessed of a healthful, saving, purifying power that is needed everywhere. The basest sensualist bows and worships in the presence of a pure and holy woman, and loses the power to think of such a being falling to his level. And this is the saving element that is required by the body politic, to arrest its present tendencies to complete corruption.

WOMAN AS AN ECONOMIST.

HOW SHE ASSISTS THE PRINCIPLES OF ECONOMY—THE USELESSNESS
OF THE DEVOTEES OF FASHION—HOW SOME ESTABLISHMENTS ARE
SUPPORTED—HOW FASHION IS REGARDED BY MEN OF SENSE—
DETHRONE THE GODDESS FASHION.

Woman, as a general proposition, contributes but little to the
wealth of the world by productive labor. All wealth comes from
production; it does not exist. Trade, speculation and general finance
cause special movements and distributions of wealth, but do not increase its sum total. It necessarily follows that those who are not
producers are consumers of what others produce. Under this rule
woman is' a consumer. Economy is one of the fixed principles of
the universe, and is exemplified in all the movements of nature;
there is a constant receiving and giving sustained that guarantees
the equilibrium of elemental nature, as well as its combinations in
form. Woman, as a whole, is no exception to this general law. She
performs the negative requirements of nature and, in all her relations
to mankind, sustains the equilibrium of the sexes in the general
economy.

In the human, as one of nature's representatives, we have not only
the material universe illustrated, but in the illustration is contained a
controlling mind, representative of the divine—though it be ever so
imperfect—which, being an individualized power, as such, exerts its
peculiar determining power over itself and surroundings, receiving in
return not only the gifts of material things, but also the contributions
of mind. Thus a poisonous mind exerts a certain malign influence over
all that comes within its range, just as the poisonous tree or flower gives
off its deleterious exhalations.

When the various classes of women are considered separately, and
their peculiarities and influence weighed, a vast difference is found in
the amount of their power for beneficial or deleterious effects. Especially does this obtain, when she is viewed from the point of economy.
Not only are some of these classes entirely non-productive, but rapa-
ciously consuming. In a pecuniary point of view they know no

boundary to their caprices, no limit to their extravagance, and are entirely outside the sphere of economy. To these classes we present, for special consideration, some remarks regarding their uselessness to the public welfare.

Has life any general purpose in the system of economy instituted in nature, whereby individuals spring from the original life in mass? Has woman any special sphere to fill, whereby her own and the general good should be promoted? or is she born to grow up, live and die to earth, without having added anything to its value, either materially, intellectually or morally? We gladly accord to all our sex the full measure of their usefulness—to the mother, for the number and beauty of souls she has individualized; to the sister, for all the sympathy she has expended in allaying the trials and suffering of humanity; to the daughter, for all the tenderness bestowed upon the aged and infirm, and to them all, for everything done, in the cause of general progression. Many have labored earnestly, devoutly, devotedly, whose names will live through centuries. To them all honor the ages can confer belongs. The only cause for regret is, that their number is so few. Shame upon us that it is so.

The other extreme is represented by the woman of fashion. Her allotment in the scale of use is a difficult one to make. She is neither the willing, health-giving mother, the generous, whole-souled sister, nor the tender, assiduous daughter. The woman of fashion has no time for the display of these weaknesses that mar the marble contour she adopts. Her heart is steeled to every inherent womanly sentiment, and her entire thought devoted to garnishing and bedecking the exterior. In her estimation, it is of much greater importance to pass through the world under full spread of sail than to give any care to the character of her ballast. In her philosophy, externals cover, in more than material matters, the nakedness of the individual. If she be perfect in appearance, of what consequence is the shallowness of her mind, which she permits no one to measure; or the depravity of her soul, which no one can see?

What does the woman of fashion do for the world? She begins and ends by deceiving it in part, and herself wholly. Walk up Broadway and count the windows wherein are exposed for sale huge, vile bunches of hair, tortured into all conceivable, unnatural shapes, to transform the natural beauty of the head to a hideous, affected thing. The amount expended on these outrages upon common sense, alone, would educate and render comfortable every child of distress and poverty. What right have you, Woman of Fashion, to thus consume wealth, while children in the next street are crying for bread? Your laces and diamonds, and other superfluous articles of ornamentation which you filch from the public welfare, seeking thereby to hide your deformities or to add to your attractions, would mitigate all the distress that stalks among us, with pale, wan cheek, tearful eye and bleeding feet. The general economy of the universe will hold you responsible for all these inequalities.

How many fortunes have you squandered, homes made desolate, and husbands driven to distraction in the pursuit of your insatiable desire for dress? and how many, when the purses of your husbands or fathers have failed to furnish what you require, and would have, have sold yourselves to others to obtain it? Demand of those who know—of the keepers of houses of prostitution and assignation of New York—then confirm their testimony by that of our police! They will declare unreservedly and positively, that in the insane love for dress, they find their support.

Go behind this more prominent form of prostitution, to that prac-ticed under the garb of marriage, and you will find immense establish-ments, complete and luxurious in their appointments, supported by the dishonor of their mistresses. To such an extent does the love of dress and display lead women to prostitute themselves, that fashion is becom-ing a stench in the nostrils of every one of her sex who values purity and devotion to her family more than the display of fashionable toi-lets and equipages, which, purchased by her own desecration, destroys all that is holy in marriage.

Every new movement made in dress is to render the concealed reality more deceptive. Calves, hips and breasts are padded to make the form more deceptively voluptuous, and thereby to appeal with more direct force to the passions of man. So notorious has this condi-tion become, that men are beginning to beware of women, and to hesi-tate to make them wives, not knowing whether the forms they present themselves in are natural or artificial. This and the knowledge of the expense of a fashionable wife, are deterring thousands from marrying. It is man who will not and woman who cannot. Woman has still to learn that men of sense most admire due regard for personal appearance, when combined with attractions of the mind and heart. Capacity of mind before profusion of dress, and intellectual attainment before knowledge of the latest styles, are always recommendations to the con-sideration of every man who should be desired for a husband. A rich mind will always command respect and admiration, though it be clothed in the greatest simplicity; a barren soul always merits contempt, though it be decked with all the fineries fashion can invent.

Fashion, then, is one of the direct inducements to prostitution, and is so testified of by all who are competent to testify; and when practiced to gratify an insane desire for display, it is in its most debasing form, for these votaries carry their pernicious influence into the bosom of their families, and outrage all the delicate sensibilities of relationship, besides entailing no one can tell how great curses upon their children. The damnation of a common prostitute begins and ends with herself and abettors, but private prostitution entails untold miseries upon all who come within, or belong to, the sphere of its influence. If the first can, by any stretch of imagination, be considered a "necessary evil" for man, the last is a burning shame upon the name of woman, to the mitigation of which every possible effort should be directed.

No more direct attack upon this condition could be made than to dethrone the Goddess Fashion. Let every woman—and every man who comprehends the situation ever so little—remember that she owes it to her daughter to demand of others, and to practice herself, such reform in dress as shall put it beyond the pale of decency to indulge as those do who devote themselves entirely to the pursuit of fashion. Demand and practice artistic simplicity that shall contribute to ease, comfort and health, and which will permit you to follow any of the new vocations that are to be opened for your competition: present modes, in many of them, would be impracticable, while the multiplicity of their requirements would be simply ridiculous if fully practiced.

A wide field for reform can here be opened. How many are there possessed of sufficient honesty, purity and devotion to your sex's interest to step forward and take the initiatory? Thousands will follow a courageous lead, and tens of thousands will bless it when it is once made. In such action the satisfaction may be felt of knowing that it is a movement in accordance with the general order of nature, which commands economy in all things; of becoming the benefactors of our sex and the admiration of the other, and of being a living embodiment of a true, natural woman, who deems it disgraceful to appear to be what she is not.

A single extract from the diary of the late Mrs. Dr. Lozier expresses the sentiment of every true, noble and pure-hearted woman. She says: "A wearisome day shopping. I pity the votaries of dress, if the thought they give to it, and time and money, are as empty of happiness to them as to me. Father, keep my heart pure and my eye single!"

WOMAN AS THE COMPANION.

HER FAILURE TO INTEREST MAN—MAN ADVANCES, WOMAN STANDS
STILL—HOME LOSING ITS ATTRACTIONS—THE DISTANCE BETWEEN
THE SEXES—THE CAUSE OF IT SUGGESTED.

Were women trained to business pursuits from childhood, as men
are, the largest successes in business would be obtainable by them.
Because they are not thus educated for any line of occupation they
remain through life complete failures, so far as practical avocations are
concerned. Woman appears upon the scene of life as a commercial
nonentity, passes through all its changes, and disappears, considering
herself a success if she has been so fortunate as to have amused man,
so that his leisure moments have passed cheerfully. Of late years she
is even failing to do this. There is a growing preferment on his part for
his club, his billiards, his chess, his anything, so that he is removed from
the society of those who, failing to interest, amuse or instruct, become
actual bores upon his sensitive patience.

When man returns from his regular daily cares and duties, he seeks
such amusement and recreation as will divert his mind from them; or
such companions as can assist him in solving some business or financial problem he is engaged upon. Nine chances in ten he finds neither
in the limits of his family; failing here, in what he most desires, anything, anywhere, is an acceptable substitute. It is a general rule, that
if one finds those he should naturally go to for advice incapable of giving it, he accepts it from others still more incapable.

The minds of all men, everywhere, are being roused into a more
comprehensive state of action. They are daily brought into contact
with the progressive ideas and thoughts of the world, which continually
modify their opinions, views, and even their methods of thought, so that
those they associate with at home, who are debarred these advantages.
or are slow to obtain them, lose the capacity to any longer attract,

These advantages are obtainable by certain classes of women who mingle largely with the world. They imbibe its inspirations, acquire its reasons and adopt its conclusions, and are pretty thoroughly competent to convince the husband that his family is behind the times, especially when he is already too painfully aware of it. Men in this respect are so thoughtlessly unjust; they make no allowance for lack of opportunity ; they simply take the fact. They do not consider while they are constantly engaged with a continuous change of circumstances, each one of which develops some new thought, illustrates some new idea or demonstrates some mooted question, that their families are shut up at home, away from all the world, except those who are in like conditions. And so it comes, that man is better amused and more wisely instructed away from home than at home.

Acknowledging to herself the loss of the power of home attractions for man, it is not to be wondered that woman is attempting the games man plays at, nor that her success is immense when so employed. It is quite to be expected that they should assemble in secret conclave to discuss their grievances and to provide remedies. Equally so, that they should organize clubs in satirical spirit, at which they drink their tea and lemonade, and under its exhilarating influence "do" the last sensation—perhaps project a new one. Nor is it very surprising, that organizations having in view still more general male practices, should be found existing in the very heart of fashionable society. In these various ways and numerous others, women are successfully managing to imitate man. True, such things have not obtained to any considerable extent, though quite sufficiently so to indicate the direction they are inclined to take to be revenged—that is the spirit—upon man, for failing to longer be amused by the hereditary customs of their fathers. One important point woman seems to have totally ignored, and this is, that as the conditions of men's minds develop toward comprehensiveness, they require equal proportionate development in all their surroundings from which they expect recreation.

Thus the distance between man and woman, as the husband and wife, is gradually widening, and the home of the family every year becomes less and less the central point of attraction for all concerned. This appears a most grievous fact, unless regarded strictly philosophically. It indicates a revolution in domestic life, such as the world has never known. Does woman comprehend whither she is floating? Does she realize that as a sex she is becoming estranged from man? Does she understand what estrangement of the sexes means for her? If, as

a sex, woman is content to remain in political bondage—if she is willing
to remain the mere appendage of man, with no individuality outside of
wifely submission, such as was commended by Paul—would it not be
wise in her to make better preparation for that sphere? Should she
not make such progress in it as would be in accordance with the general progress of the world, so that she should be capable of making
home minister to all man's requirements? However indefinite man's
desires regarding woman may be—and that they are indefinite his course
indicates but too well—he does not wish a mere cipher for a wife, but a
companion, capable and willing for all occasions. If the reality could
be known, though he is far from confessing it, he would honor the
woman who could fill his position during his absence.

So much for the condition! What of the cause?

If we do not widely err in tracing effects back to their cause, the
chief thing that has caused and is causing domestic infelicity has never
yet been touched—has been shut out from sight and consideration. It
is the growing aversion on the part of women to bearing children.
The means they resort to for their prevention is sufficient to disgust
every natural man, and to cause him to seek the companionship of
those who have no fear in this regard. Every wife should be wise
enough to know what the result of this course must be. She should
remember it is not in harmony with the general processes of nature,
and that it must induce conditions unfavorable to her continuance as
the sufficient attraction for the man who has chosen her from among
the whole. The trite saying that "there are two sides to all questions" is very applicable in the inharmonious domestic relations of the
sexes. Man does not wander from home, wife, and perhaps children,
for no cause. There is a beginning to everything short of absolute
existence. The basis of the relations of the sexes is in the fact that
they are male and female, the union between whom is requisite for
the purposes of reproduction. For this end they are male and female,
and for this are they brought into the relationship in which so much
unhappiness now exists. Here is the primal attraction, and here must
we look for the primal causes of separation. With the profoundest
regard for the gravity and delicacy of the question, we ask wives to examine themselves, to see whether the first cause of discontent on the
part of husbands, which inclines them to seek other female society, is
not their unnatural conduct regarding their special maternal functions?

WOMAN AS THE REFORMER.

NO RESTRICTIONS IN THIS SPHERE—WHY SHOULD THERE BE IN OTHERS?
—TURKEY AND UTAH—THE BASIS OF REFORM.

In no department of civilization can woman exert so much influence as in that usually denominated reform, though, strictly speaking there is no meaning in the term. In this specific department her lacking equality does not militate so greatly against her general usefulness as in most other spheres. To all the requirements of this situation she is allowed admission, and is recognized in her true relations therein.

When woman is herself the unfortunate, who lingers among the lower and barbaric forms of civilization, it is true that her degradation seems of greater depth than that of man does, when sunk in equal filth; it is also true, that greater effort is required to encourage her to grow out of such conditions than man usually requires. We have often thought that this grows out of the fact that the scales of justice in which society weighs woman are fearfully loaded against her, and that double depth of iniquity in man does not weigh so heavily, nor damn him so much, as one-half the depth in woman. A single false step, socially, is sufficient to stain woman's whole after life, and to exclude her most rigorously from the society of woman; but man may continuously mingle with the society constituted of those thus excluded with impunity.

The verdict of society is, that man does not become defiled by contact with impurity, but that woman does, and when once defiled, the stain is too deep to be ever eradicated. It is not man, however, who is thus inconsistent—who thus proposes one rule for himself and another totally different for woman. It is herself that does it, but the condition itself comes from quite another direction. It comes from the inequalities of the sexes. It comes because woman is virtually the dependent—the slave of man. Though it may not be so regarded, a strict analysis pronounces her the slave; for she has no determining power over her own condition. She cannot make or unmake a law she finds she suffers from; she cannot determine what shall be the penalty that shall affix to any crime she shall commit, or that she shall suffer at the hands of man; she cannot even accord to herself the rights to pos- sess property nor to deal in or dispose of it if possessed. What better than a slave is such a condition as this? Ask yourselves, women, and see if this is not so, though it must be confessed the condition has been draped with many allurements to those who are willing to remain non- entities in the affairs of the world, in place of possessing a noble inde- pendence, and the right to be the arbiter in their own condition.

If we mistake not most seriously, the basis of the work of reform has not been reached as yet by the majority of women. How can those who are in a subjugated condition expect to wield the power of a re- former, either in matters pertaining to that condition or in those outside of it? Would you look for reformers in a Turkish harem, or among the wives of the Mormons? And why not? It is because they are in a condition only worse in degree than all other women are. Are harems confined to the Turks or Mormons to Utah? It must be remembered that it takes all the rounds of a ladder to form it complete, and that those of the elevated part are only higher in degree than the lower, and that all are rounds of the same ladder. So, too, is it with the condition of women, viewed as a whole. What is the difference, except in de- gree, between the women of Utah and Turkey and those of the rest of the world? They are all the subject of conditions over which they have no control, and are therefore everywhere the same.

The work of the reformer, to be successful, must begin by remov- ing this condition of subserviency. All women, everywhere, must have the same rights, both as individuals and as parts of society—neither of which is possessed by them now—as all men have, with whom they as- sociate; there must be an equality, an operative equality, a constructive equality, between the sexes, before either man or woman can obtain a fair *entree* upon that race for perfection which it is the heart's desire of all to obtain. Do you not think that a vigorous attack would be made upon many of the existing imperfections of society, were our halls of legislation occupied by the best representatives of both sexes? And here lies the basis of all reform. Legislation should be conducted by the representatives of the whole of society, male and female. Women, to become powerful as reformers, must first become the political equals of those they seek to reform. To obtain their equality, it must be demanded by the voice of the majority. To teach the majority the necessity of making the demand, is the beginning of reform, and to show women the actual condition they are submitting to, is one of the principal duties of those who recognize the relations of causes to effects, or rather the common order of the universe in its march from elemental conditions to those represented by perfected combinations of elements, which is continually pursued onward, and never by retreat. We, therefore, enter our declaration, that all who are opposed to the political equality of woman, are opposed to the first principles of progress, and are therefore enemies to the race.

INDEPENDENCE OR DEPENDENCE, WHICH?

WOMAN BEHIND IN THE GENERAL RACE FOR ADVANCEMENT—HER
FORMER POSITION BEING GRADUALLY INVADED—THE FUTURE
OF HOUSEKEEPING—WOMEN OF INTELLECT MUST HAVE OCCU-
PATION—SHALL SHE LONGER BE HELD A VIRTUAL NONENTITY?

In this age of progress, wherein rapid strides are being made in all
branches of civilization, woman seems to be about the only constituent
feature which is devoid of the general spirit that controls. All the elements of society are becoming more distinctly individualized with increasing heterogeneity. Its lines of demarkation, while increasing nu-
merically, become more distinct. The whole tendency is to individual
independence and mutual dependence. It is most true that in the
aid which progress receives from peoples, that the female element is but
poorly represented, but its effects are sufficiently obvious and diffusive
to demonstrate, even to her, that there must be a forward movement
made by the sex, else it will be left entirely too far in the rear to perform
even an unimportant part in the great wants that the immediate future
will develop.

The wife was formerly the housekeeper; she is becoming less and
less so every day. Many of the duties that once devolved upon her,
are now performed by special trades. Each branch of housewifery is
coming to be the basis of a separate branch of business. Schools perform all the duties of education that once devolved upon the mother,
and tailors and dress-makers absorb the labor of the wardrobe. The
grocer and the baker pretty nearly supply the table, while the idea of

furnishing meals complete, is rapidly gaining acceptance. Thus, one by one, the duties of the housewife are being taken from her, by the better understanding and adaptation of principles of general economy. While the revolution is in progress, the preparatory steps to co-operative housekeeping are being taken. Thousands live at one place and eat at another, where once such practice was unknown. Dining saloons are increasing more rapidly than any other branch of business, and more transient meals are eaten every day. The result of this will be a division of living, under the two systems represented by the two classes of hotels—the *table d'hote* and the *a la carte*. The residence portion of our cities will be converted into vast hotels, which will be arranged and divided for the accomodation of families of all sizes. A thousand people can live in one hotel, under one general system of superintendence, at much less expense than two hundred and fifty families of four members each, in as many houses and under as many systems. As a system of economy, this practice is sure to prevail, for progress in this respect is as equally marked as in attainment, and, if we mistake not, is of a higher order. To obtain more effect from a given amount of power, is a higher branch of science than to obtain the same by increasing the power. To lessen resistance is better than to increase power, and on this principle progress in the principles of living is being made toward co-operation.

Allowing that the practice will become general, what will become of the "special sphere" of woman, that is painted in such vivid colors by the opponents of the extension of female privileges? Are the powers of women to be wasted upon vain frivolities so widely practised now, where this principle is already operating, or are they to be cast in some useful channel—some honorable calling? Is fashion to consume the entire time of women of the immediate future, or shall they become active members of the social body, not only forming a portion of its numbers, but contributing their share to the amount of results to be gained? True, the beginning of this practice is forcing women into wider fields of usefulness; forcing them without preparation into competition with man, who has been trained to industry from youth—a vast disparity, over which the complaint of unequal pay is sometimes raised without real cause.

Does woman foresee what these things are to lead to, or does she prefer to remain blind to the tendencies of progress in this regard? It is evident to every mind, not wilfully blind, that woman is gradually merging into all the employments of life. They are being ·

2

driven to it by the force of circumstances, coming from new developments. It is a necessity. Occupation they must have; for not all women
even will be content to lead useless lives. This condition is gradually
increasing, both in volume and extent, and, with a persistency which
overcomes all opposition custom offers, it proclaims its intentions. Why
cannot its drift be recognized as a matter of course, and all provisions
made to help the cause along? Women who do not perceive these
things, from habitual blindness to all that usefulness indicates, may be
excused for their supineness; but men, who are habitually provident,
stand condemned of inconsistency for all the opposition manifested to
the course events will pursue.

In consideration of the fact that woman is entering the active
sphere of life, and is every day widening this sphere, can she sit in utter quiescence, saying she has no desire to establish herself as an element of power, politically? In this she voluntarily acknowledges her
inferiority, and her willingness to remain the political slave, which is
but a shade removed from the slavery that cost the country so much
life to extinguish.

However much man may at present resist the bold demands of the
few, now calling for political equality, were the sex, as a whole, to rouse
itself into a comprehension of the situation and its prophecies, with the
determination to assert equality of privilege, in the control of that in
which they have an equality of interest, he would not dare refuse.
Let the question be put home to yourselves in the light of rising events,
and considered with calmness and wisdom. Are you willing to remain
a political nonentity, a dependent upon the consideration of those who
do possess political rights, and be subservient to masters of others' making? Shall you not the rather demand political equality, basing it on
an equality of interest, in the results to be obtained through the exercise of political rights? The first means continued dependence; the
last means the beginning of independence. These are the questions.
Consider them.

WOMAN'S SPHERE.

GLITTERING GENERALITIES AND TERRIFIC PHANTASIES—THE PRINCI-
PLES WHICH CAUSE REFORM—WHAT NEGRO EQUALITY MEANT—
WHAT EQUALITY FOR WOMAN MEANS—DOES THE PAST TEACH ANY
LESSONS?—WHAT PROPERTY OF SOCIETY DOES WOMAN REPRESENT?
—IS SHE SOMETHING OR NOTHING?—ABSOLUTE MONARCHY.

The glittering generalities which surround this phrase, and cast
over it such impenetrable mysteries, such inscrutable relations and
phantomatic beauties, are in danger of being analyzed. All mysteries
fear the touch of whatever will rend the veil that conceals their true
character. Most formidable assumptions vanish before the scrutiny of
reason. Terrific phantasies become pleasing realities when bereft of
their allegorical shroudings, and the most improbable theories plain
facts, when reduced to practice.

The hue and cry of negro equality, made by those who knew its
shallowness, to influence the thoughtless, is now found to have been a
myth. They would have persuaded us that, if slavery was abolished,
every white daughter would be compelled to mate with a negro, and
that every son would incline to color. Slavery is dead, and the negro
remains to all purposes the same as he was, except that he is free. He
has the rights of a citizen ; but the privileges of society he must obtain
as others obtain them—by capacity, adaptability and attractability. If
your sons and daughters incline to color, it is not because black has
been raised to the dignity of white, but because white has descended to
the level of black, and for this, if blame is to attach, it should belong
to those who had their youth in charge.

The cry of equality is now generally conceded to have been a fic-
tion of the first water. It has been abandoned as too improbable for
even a burlesque. All who were engaged in raising it acknowledge the
issue dead, and that the negro who in 1820 was little better than a beast

—a fit subject for the block and lash—casts his ballot the same as whites, to express his political preferences. Fifty years of strife accomplished this for him. His advocates were not from his own ranks. Principles of justice and common right, singled them from the more favored class. They were those within whose souls the principles of freedom were predominant, which brought them forth to battle for the common rights of humanity. All forms of persecutions were hurled against them. They were laughed at, scorned and stoned. Still they lifted their voices for freedom for all ; and nature, ever true to herself and consistent, decided that the new should supplant the old. Ever since creation the same process has produced similar results.

Has the enfranchisement of the negro any lesson for the conservatives of the world ? or must the same battle be fought for every step of general progress ? There are those who still think they can bend the common order of the universe, to meet their selfish and impossible conclusions. Therefore, those who are now striking for enlarged spheres of action, must expect to encounter the same opposition that has been offered to all previous forward movements. Every revolution that ever occurred brought into positions of control, more and more of the sum total of the people. Once an Alexander and a Cæsar dictated to the world. Later a Napoleon attempted it and failed. In this nineteenth century the voice of every son and daughter must be heard and acknowledged a sovereign power.

What is woman's sphere? Is it to be marked and defined by others than herself and nature? Does man inherit from Paul the authority he seeks to maintain over her, so that she shall not have the privilege of speaking her wants? Does woman, or does she not, form a part of the body of society? Is it male and female, or only male? Is it her sphere to shrink before the dicta of man, and bow in submission to his will? Is it hers to be ruled and bound by laws he shall compel her to ? Has she no individual authority except that which he may graciously accord to her ? The horse and ox are free to enjoy the privileges their masters allow them—to eat, drink and sleep, and when not required for use to roam within the limits marked for them. And this is woman's sphere! She is free to do everything, except the very thing that determines her condition. She is as much a slave as the negro was. He had the power of persuasion, but no right to demand. So, too, have women. Have they aught else? Can they say that this or that shall be thus or thus? Try it and be convinced that you have no more real power than the negro had. It is said that there are those who desire to remain in this condition, caressing the hands which bind them, and receiving consideration from those who regard them as only fit for such a condition. It does not seem possible that either they or you comprehend the situation. We would not be other than respectful to our self-constituted lords and masters; but we must first respect our selves. If we mistake not, charity, no more than other virtues, should begin at home. We have never elected that man should fashion governments to rule us. By what right does he do so, and then refuse us hearing?

Man's sphere is just what he chooses to make it within the limitations of nature. We demand that woman's shall be what she shall elect to make it, subject only to the same limitations, and our demand is entitled to the same respect that man's possession receives. We claim, that when we come before you and ask a voice in legislation and administration, which you have reserved to yourselves, that you have no other than the right of might—the tyrant's right—to deny us. So far as you do deny us, just so far are you tyrants and we slaves. All the coloring it may be glossed over with can make it nothing better, nor can it be made to appear, that we are aught but your subjects, the same as a people are the subjects of an absolute monarch—the only difference is that he is one while you are multitudes. He makes the laws for his people; you make them for us. They are obliged to submit; so are we. Where is the difference, except in degree? We claim, on the contrary, that we have rights, as individuals, which you can neither give nor take away. You may prevent our making use of them. Just so far as you do are you just and we free; or you tyrants and we slaves.

PREJUDICE vs. JUSTICE.

THE ROAD THE REFORMER HAS TO TRAVEL—THE CHARGE OF "EAT-
ING WITH PUBLICANS AND SINNERS"—"MOTES" AND "BEAMS"—
DENUNCIATION, RECRIMINATION AND BOMBASTIC DISPLAY—MAN
NOT WILLINGLY PART WITH ANY PRIVILEGE—MOST HONORABLE WILL
EXPONENTS OF THE RIGHT SPIRIT.

It is but the old story, so oft repeated, that those who have the hardi-
hood and devotion to go out into the world, the representatives and advocates of convictions of right, are met, not by reason and common sense,
nor yet by any plea of impropriety as to time and place, but by wholesale
denunciation, or such sweeping accusations as are believed to be, and are,
sufficient to overwhelm all, except such souls as alone undertake these
steps. Probably most who thus attempt what, to the initiated, appear
impossibilities, are not at first conscious of the storms they must encounter, and step boldly forth with no preparations to battle against its fury,
nor protect themselves from being swept hurriedly away by its ruthless
torrents. More especially is this true, when any appear as the advocate
of what, if triumphant, shall interfere with some time-honored institution, custom, privilege or creed. During all the past this has been continually exemplified. Even Christ was vilified for eating with "publicans and sinners." Unfortunately, all are not the possessors of that
ready wisdom that can retort that "he that is without sin among
you cast the first stone." Still more unfortunate is it for the present,
that the accusing multitude, if so rebuked in these times, would not
retire from the presence of the judge, covered with shame for its unwarrantable usurpation of the right of accusation, though as fully convicted
as the Jews of old were. They do not realize that, though not defiled

A

by the exact sin it accuses their would-be victims of, they have others still more damning or contemptible, of which they stand convicted before their God.

It were well for all who have any desire to lay claim to progressive ideas or to Christian precepts, to examine themselves well to see if they have not a "beam" in their own eyes, before attempting to cast out the "mote" they think to have discovered in their neighbor's. Little does the reckless asserter of scandalous reports know what he does, when he bandies a name upon his lips, with such connections as would traduce purity itself, and throw a mantle of distrust over all its actions. When driven to his authority it often eludes him, and he is fain to declare he must have dreamed it. But he has repeated the curse to thoughtless ears, and these have spread it among the eager crowd, and thus it comes that those who have endeavored to live the principles that have developed in their souls are adrift upon the waves of society, bereft of all the necessary means to gain the port desired.

Thus are the pioneers in the cause of a common equality met by those who certainly are not their superiors in any way, except in their knowledge of, and as participators in, the vice and immorality of the times. All of the members of this class of opposers are possessed of colored glasses, through which they view the presumptuous petitioners. Of course, they are all "black" in some sense, and are straightway thus proclaimed. Do they ever meet the petitions presented with answering reason. Oh, they have no reasons to offer, and therefore must resort to the only line of reasoning the blockhead and the blackguard have—to denunciation, recrimination and bombastic display of self-importance, thus endeavoring to crush their petitioners out by the very weight of their displeasure. "What!" they say, "you equal to us? Preposterous! ridiculous! absurd! Equal to us, who have these many long years held you in complete subjection? The presumption of your claim is too barefaced to allow us to think it is made in sincerity, and the best you can do is, to get you back to your washtubs and needles before the compassion we now have for your imbecility is turned into vinegar by your persistence. Get you away before we are forced to call our lackeys, who are our equals, to 'put you out,' for out we are determined you shall go. We already have to share our rights with too many. Foreigners who come to us from abroad with the determination to become citizens, we cannot keep in a condition to do our bidding. The negro we are forced to vote with, do jury duty with, sit in the halls of Congress with. We cannot divide our spoils anew with you, for to do so is to take the larger half of all we have remaining. Whatever

your claims may be, whatever of justice they may be founded on, whatever of argument you may support them by, we will not consider them.
If there are those among us so weak and foolish as to entertain your demands, and bring them before us, and thus compel us into action upon
them, why, we must perforce vote you Nay, and decide the matter at
once, for it is useless to waste time in listening to arguments, when we
are determined not to be convinced."

This course is the only one that can be followed by those who, having power, are determined not to part with it. As for arguments, there
are none to offer. The same line of opposition is practiced regarding
position in all matters heretofore held exclusively by the "Lords of
Creation." If any innovations are attempted upon preoccupied grounds,
straightway the forces are combined to expel the invader. All manner of practices known to the "sharps" are attempted; and money
even, which they all part with so unwillingly, is freely offered, if *some
one* will only "make up" *something* that will effectually extinguish
them. Failing in everything else, schemes are planned to work upon
the points of weakness that it has been discovered they possess, and
their own sex is played against them to entangle them in some net set
to catch them, or to lead them into some quagmire in which they shall
sink beyond hope of escape. Most honorable opponents, you put your
talents to most worthy uses! How sweet your dreams must be when
you are *so* just! The time will most surely come when your hypocrisy
will be unmasked, and you be made to appear before the bar of public
opinion as you now appear before the bar of Divine Justice.

Public opinion is not entirely unregenerate, and wofully will you
repent it, if you rely fully upon it for your continuous justification. It
may justify you to-day, but beware, lest to-morrow it shall reverse its
decision, and condemn you for the prejudiced usurper of rights of sex
which you really are. We ask every conscientious man to be *more*
just, and not to wait the time when he must be. Hear our demands;
listen to our arguments; treat our attempts to maintain a womanly independence in the same spirit they are made; and permit us to think
that we at least have the *right* to support ourselves, if we do not all
choose to make use of it. Do away with your unwarrantable prejudices,
and extend us the right hand of fellowship, the same as you do to many
whom we believe to be far less worthy of it than we are. We do not
ask favor. We only desire justice, and that equality of privilege which
is due us from the equality of interest we have in the results to flow
from its possession.

WHAT DOES THE SIXTEENTH AMENDMENT IMPLY?

THE WEAPONS USED AGAINST ITS ADVOCATES—THE OBLIGATIONS OF
WOMAN—THE REDEEMING QUALITIES OF WOMAN.

To hear the terrible anathemas that are continually hurled against
the advocates of woman's rights, the uninitiated would suppose the
proposition involves the most radical and unreasonable changes in the
present order of society. Especially, if one listens to the imprecations
called down upon the movement by the representatives of "the old time
religion," would he imagine its advocates were from that region so
familiar to their vernacular, where the devil reigns supreme, the precise
locality of which, however, they fail to inform us of. It is enough that
it is of the devil, and as such it is worthy of the denunciation it receives
from them. But how far does this opposition meet any single issue of
the question involved? Let the question be analyzed, and what does it
contain that it should arouse such bitter vituperation and should bring
down upon its advocates such wholesale denunciation? We ask simply
to be received and acknowledged as one of the constituent parts of
society, and as such to be admitted to its counsels, and, with man, to
be responsible for its conditions.

As it now is, woman is subjugated, is utterly powerless to do other
than as her master shall direct; and whether this involves the reception of brute force from him, or a semi-acquiescence in the things that
he demands from her, it matters not, the principle is the same. And in
whatever sphere of life woman may be, this domination is the power
that determines her condition. In some of the cities of the Eastern ·
States, especially Massachusetts and Rhode Island, a very large proportion of the population is female. Lowell and Lawrence, Pawtucket
and Blackstone are good illustrations. In what way can it be shown

that the factory girls of these cities are free—are in a condition very far removed from slavery? There they toil day after day, for weeks, months and years, and finally die without ever fulfilling the best mission of woman, and why? Would this be so very long were woman raised to the level and dignity of an equality with man? Are they destitute of the common sentiments of womanhood, among which maternity stands prominently forth?

Another not commonly known fact has a powerful bearing in forming a judgment of the character of woman. It is true, as a general proposition, that the woman who does content herself to work, work, work for her sustenance and for that of those dependent upon her, prefers to do this rather than resort to that far easier way many do. The laboring woman is the virtuous woman. All laboring women are, as a rule, virtuous women. It would be a source of the greatest astonishment could it be generally known and appreciated how much real labor woman does. It is true that it is that kind of labor which does not bring the subject into special notice, nor such return in money or position as renders her in any sense, the equal of the man laborer. Nevertheless it is certain that nearly, if not quite, one-half of all labor that is accomplished is performed by women. There are many instances among the wealthy where the women of the family do nothing. On the contrary how many are there among the very poor, where the woman of the family is its support; where the men spend all their time and money, and often much of that earned by the women, in debauch and drink. It will not do to look only on one side of a question that is under consideration, if a just decision is desired, and hence it is that we declare, that a sufficient proportion of the actual labor of the world is performed by woman, and to demand for her, in the name of justice, a substantial equality—an equality that shall enable her to determine her own condition.

The union of the sexes is the natural condition, and man and woman should enter it from an equal dignity of position and equally voluntarily. Society should be so that no woman should feel obliged to marry or connect herself with man for the object of support, and she should be in such condition that she should never enter upon the new relation, from any other reasons than natural law, and from the fact that there exists a mutual attraction. A more momentous question is involved in this apparently simple matter than the superficial ever supposed possible. Let the question be proposed, Whence come all these puny, imperfect, even idiotic children the world is filled with? They come simply from the relations existing between the father and mother which should have prevented their union. Not only are diseases of the body engendered, but the still worse infirmities of the heart, soul and mind result therefrom.

Thus it is that disease, crime and all other evils the world is subjected to, are perpetually resurrected in each succeeding generation. The first step to be taken for the removal and cure of this condition, is, to extend equality to such women as desire it and to show those who yet prefer to remain subjugated to the domination and rule of man, that theirs is, in fact, the condition of the slave, willing though it be. What man is there who would surrender his independence and the possibilities of his condition to become to woman what all wives now are to men? Would he become dependent upon her he would marry, surrender to her his rights and the rights to preferment which are prophetically every man's? It is becoming somewhat the rule now, that men do not care to be bound to a wife. What will result from such a procedure if continued? Society may well stop and consider where the wrong lies, that is engendering all these false and unphilosophic conditions; it may affect surprise and hold up its hands in holy horror, but it nevertheless comes from one fact, and that fact is, that one-half the world is subjugated to the other half, and has no voice in the general conduct of affairs, by which its parts become either to itself or society, necessary and important factors, except in the matter of obedience and labor.

What would be the legitimate result of the admission of woman to the ballot? Would it necessarily or probably lead to any worse filling of office than now obtains? Would there, could there, be more general corruption exhibited in legislation and in the administration of law, by people chosen, by men and women promiscuously, than there is now on the part of those chosen by men alone. To assert such a result, or to affect to believe that such a result would follow, is ridiculously absurb. Whatever depths of degradation members of the sex have fallen to, the sex, as a whole, is possessed of a purifying and exalting power that man is devoid of, and in debarring this power from entering into political arenas, they are depriving themselves of an element of salvation ; and they will some day repent of having done so.

WILL WOMEN ACCEPT THE CONSE-
QUENCES OF EQUALITY?

EQUALITY IN MILITARY DUTY—NON-COMBATANTS OF ALL KINDS,
SHALL THEY LOSE THEIR CITIZENSHIP?—INTELLECTUAL WOMEN
VS. THE IGNORANT MILLION.

It is frequently advanced as an argument or rather set off against
giving woman the right of the ballot, that if she votes she should be
subject to draft for military duty. Well, we have no objection. All
we would ask is that when the conscription is made, none may be accepted save those who are really physically competent. This number
would be found so small that we doubt if the whole State of New York
could furnish a regiment. But in case of a call for volunteers, there is
not a doubt if women were permitted to serve, a great many more
would come forward at their country's call than would be found able
to carry arms. Let women do as they please. Restrict them by no
laws that would not equally bind men. Give to both men and women
the guide of a properly educated and developed conscience, and there
will be no need of arbitrary laws binding either to their separate duties.
They who contend to the contrary prove themselves practical infidels
and unbelievers in the Christianity they profess. Christianity gives
free scope, and tolerance needs no law to enforce its precepts. We
may engraft Christianity with civil institutions as they exist, but never
insist that those institutions are Christianity. We would " render unto
Cæsar the things that are Cæsar's and to God the things that are God's."
Never insist that God and Cæsar shall be united or are one.

If women should not vote because they are non-combatants, then
all non-combatants should be deprived of the ballot. All infirm and

disabled men, from any cause, should be debarred from all legislative and civil representation by ballot. John Randolph, of Roanoke; Alexander Stephens, of Georgia, and many other men of giant minds but weak physical developments, would, by this rule, be consigned to what has been considered woman's sphere.

What is woman's sphere? 'Twould be difficult to define its limits. Is it where nature places her? Then let us not insist that those who are not fitted by nature for marriage and maternity *shall be* wives and mothers, or submit to the old maid's fate—the tolerated sister-in-law, meekly wielding the crochet needle.   Let each individual woman, as well as each individual man, seek her being's highest, noblest, truest, best development. Let her do the duty that lies nearest to her, whatever that duty may be; and if our great republic and the governments of the world give her the right of self-representation by the ballot, let her not shrink from the responsibilities involved in her new political privilege. Let her prepare herself for her enfranchisement by education, self-discipline and self-abnegation, not like a fool, rush in where angels should fear to tread.

The ballot for women ? Most assuredly, yes. As they are mentally and physically the equals of men, why should they not be so politically? The question answers itself. That answer embraces the fact that women, although but the mental and physical equals of men, are also their moral superiors. The cynical skepticism born of *cliques* and clubs and smoking-rooms may have a word here, but the teachings of experience light our judgment and confirm our faith. White women are certainly as capable of exercising discrimination as are the negro and heathen voters who now overrun the land; and they are fully as intelligent. If they are really inferior, why do men hesitate to permit the self-deluded creatures to, work their own ruin by signal proofs of that lack of knowledge which is suspected in their cases only?

We are continually hearing fine speeches about justice and the necessary purification of the ballot. Now this is all sham. If one part of creation were really anxious to be just to the other part, they would commence their praiseworthy work without loss of time. The pretended fear of wives and daughters being used as mere tools in the hands of designing men, is a silly argument which does not even rise to the dignity of an excuse. Women are not necessarily obliged to accept the views of certain men as the guiding principles of their lives. They are quite capable of forming opinions, and doubtless could maintain them publicly, and that, too, without outraging any of the decencies of humanity or civilization. They need pursue none of those courses which brand some of our greatest men with indellible infamy. Their follies need never degenerate into vices, and their should be no reason why their moral tone must necessarily become so lowered and degraded as to disgust their fellow beings. By persevering unselfishness and devotion they might accomplish their great mission of regeneration. There could never be any necessity for them to encourage license and disorder by making of themselves but poor copies of very bad originals.

We are fully aware that this subject of female suffrage is not quite new, but it never lacks interest and can lose nothing in importance by being seriously discussed. Even the most prejudiced must admit that this claim is strongly defined and has been ably advocated. Its advancement is not prompted by a desire for the triumph of any particular political party, but simply as a means of elevating women and of immeasurably improving their condition. It remains then for the pioneers in reform to crown the edifice of political liberty by according to the importunate ones those social rights and the legal status which they claim.

Having conscientiously considered the desirability of feminine voters, let men at once inaugurate the revolution so earnestly demanded. It can but be productive of good results.

WHO ARE REPRESENTATIVE WOMEN?

WHO ARE GREAT WOMEN?—ONE SCALE OF JUSTICE FOR MEN AND ANOTHER FOR WOMEN—POLITICAL EQUALITY THE REAL BASIS OF ALL OTHER KINDS OF EQUALITY.

We ask this question, with the view to bring the minds of the people of the present to a calm consideration of what it is that constitutes representative women. We take it that the word representative means the best representatives of her sex in all general things; and that best, means those who accomplish the most for individual and general good. Napoleon once replied, that she is the greatest woman who bears the most children. We take it that a woman may be very great in this sense and still be very small in all general senses. Even in this special respect the woman who bears the greatest number of children cannot be considered the greatest woman. But if we add a modifying clause and say, that she is the greatest woman who bears the largest number of the most perfect children, we should come much nearer expressing the true greatness of woman, in this special sense, than Napoleon did.

'Tis true that the special and distinctive feature of woman, is that of bearing children, and that upon the exercise of her functions in this regard the perpetuity of the race depends. It is also true that those who pass through life, failing in this special feature of their mission, cannot be said to have lived to the best purposes of woman's life. But while maternity should always be considered the most holy of all the functions woman is capable of, it should not be lost sight of, in devotion to this, that there are as various spheres of usefulness outside of it, for woman, as there are for men outside of the marriage relation. If the same line and process of reasoning is allowed outside of the marriage relations that obtains within, then it is obvious that woman has an equal mission with man, in all things which go to make up a useful and a profitable life.

Unless woman is an inferior being in the scale of creation to man, we hold it to be a self-evident truth that she is his equal in all that pertains to life, and that any assumption of superiority over her, by man, is as purely tyrannical and arbitrary as assumption of authority by man over man is. The denial of equality then, in any sphere of·life, to woman by man, irremediably stamps him as the tyrant to the extent of such denial, and equally stamps her as the slave to the same extent. We hold it to be an undeniable and incontrovertible proposition that all the special ills which woman is the victim of, as distinguished from man, are the result of withholding from her—the denial to her—of equality in all respects.

Why is there one scale of justice in which prostitution is weighed and its representatives condemned, and scales of an entirely different balance in which licentiousness is weighed and its representatives judged? It is because the inferiority of woman in the scale of independence makes her subservient to the conditions, that she may thereby obtain what man, by his superior and self-assumed position, can obtain by different methods. She is the slave of the conditions man imposes upon her; and this is true, though perhaps in a less degree, of very many who are not in the above condition. What proportion of marriages are marriages of convenience; and what proportion of married life only differs from prostitution, by having the consent and approval of law, which can neither produce nor maintain that law, which should alone be the basis of all marriage. Why are not men prostitutes ; and why do they not live upon the sale of themselves as women do? It is because the demand for money is from the other side. Were men in the forced condition of inferiority women are, prostitution would be reversed, and men would become the prostitutes and women the respected libertines, whom no contact with man could so defile, but that they would be received and acknowledged in the best society, and she who had ruined the most men would be the special favorite among the inferior sex.

Political equality is the equality that woman lacks, the having of which will remove all those special deficiencies that place her at the foot of the scale of importance. When those who have gained independence enough, and have solved the problem of inequality, come out and demand for themselves and their sex, the right to determine

their own conditions, and for it are called all the abusive names oppo-
sers can rally and fling at them, it is but natural that these should be
hurled back in the teeth of their progenitors with a vehemence which
conscious equality must feel. Who shall speak for her who demands
the right of suffrage and say that she is not a "good woman and true?"
Such representatives of fossilized humanity ought to be well preserved,
that coming generations might look upon them and wonder that they
could have existed in the latter part of the nineteenth century. But
when we are reminded, even as jocose illustration, that there are people in certain remote counties still regularly voting for Andrew Jack-
son for President, we should not be utterly lost in amazement at the
arrogance and ignorance which denounces the woman as base and false
who makes political speeches and desires to vote.

It seems, then, that the wanting of the power to control their own
conditions, equally with man, is the want in which all the ills of the
sex, as contradistinguished from the ills of man, germinate and flourish; and that woman can never arise to a plane of equality in anything until this determining power is accorded to by those who, for
purely selfish motives, now withhold it to themselves, and make use
of the power thus arbitrarily possessed. This is the root of the evil,
and *they* are "the representative women" of the day and age who
boldly face the opposing hosts and lay the axe to the root with a re-
lentless persistence.

THE MR. TEMPLES OF SOCIETY.

PUTTY WOMEN, OR WOMEN AS IS WOMEN, WHICH? — SHALL WIVES
BE INDIVIDUALS OR MERE PUPPETS?—SENSIBLE ADVICE—WHAT
IS EXPECTED OF WOMEN.

The *Evening Telegram* of the 12th inst. contains the following :

FEMININE WOMEN.—"I think, if I marry," said Mr. Temple,
glancing across at Florence, "I shall educate my future wife to suit my
requirements. I like a feminine woman, and in our day when the gen-
tler sex compete for honors at our universities, and what not, it is time
for men who want wives in the old sense of the word, to have a school
of their own in which to educate them. Only a few days ago, I read
of single, married and widow ladies having taken degrees. I grant
there are some men who might like to marry a female M. D., but I am
not among the number, for I believe we have round corners which
need planing and polishing; and I hold that a woman's tenderness and
gentleness is the greatest safety a man has, and therefore I do not wish
her to lose her identity in Gradgrind study. Let her be well-read by
all means, but eschew competition with men. Only imagine a husband
and wife going up to the counting-house bent on the same business! We
have hardness enough to deal with daily. Why should women be educated in the same rough school? Give me, rather, a womanly wife, who
would be one with me in all my pursuits; who would sympathize with
me in all my difficulties; who would cheer me with her honest advice;
and who would beguile me from money-making by her affection ; and
not a manly woman, who would bore me with argument, weary me with
her politics, or boast of her degree.

Just so, Mr. Temple ; you are in the same fix in which all those
men are who desire to dominate over and compel women to be what
they wish, instead of what they would otherwise be. That is just

what we have been endeavoring to convince you of all this time; and now you have unwittingly exposed your true colors, and have admitted the full truth of all we have claimed, regarding the determination of man to release no part of the power he now possesses over woman, to compel her to his conditions on the one hand, and, on the other, to question their right to determine anything for themselves. If what women shall make of *themselves* when they shall have the opportunity of choosing does not happen to suit such as you, Mr. Temple, they will not only have the infinite satisfaction of being satisfied with themselves, but also of being able to provide for themselves, even if you will not condescend to marry and support them; and this, too, without being forced to the only resort unprepared women have when man fails them—to prostitution.

"I shall educate my future wife to suit my requirements." Just so, again, Mr. Temple; and this it is your right to do, if you can find so simple and weak a tool as to submit to such degradation; far be it from us to question your right to any such woman; no doubt your practices will require just such submission on the part of a wife as such willingness would imply. You want a woman "moulded" to your desires. But how about your suiting her requirements; or has she no voice, no right in the matter? Is she the thing to be picked out and used, with no reservation on her part of individual rights? Are all women to forever quietly submit to being made the docile, tractable persons your requirements indicate; or so appear to be, because they know what your requirements are? The greatest lengths of deception are practiced by women upon those who require such surrender of selfhood and womanhood, and such descent into nonentity as to submit to all your caprices, whims and passions without any choice of their own.

It may be that a large majority of women are content to forever remain "putty women," to be moulded to suit the tastes of men, but there happen to be just a few, Mr. Temple, who have individuality enough to know what they desire for themselves, a little better than you can inform them, and, withal, who have strength of purpose enough to accomplish it, even if when accomplished they shall know they will not suit the requirements of the Mr. Temples of society, who will only have for wives such as can and will bend themselves, in the very meek submission that their "requirements" demand, and who cannot endure to be "bored" with women who are capable of argument, nor wearied with those to whom politics are possible, nor humiliated by those who have attained " degrees " worthy of pride, and which may, by the faintest possibility, outshine your own.

The harems of the Turks, and tne multiplicity of Mormon wives, are held in professed contempt and abhorrence by the Mr. Temples and their "requirements;" but to our mind a more disgusting, humiliating and acquiescent servility cannot be imagined than is required by the above formula for wifely preparation. The Mr. Temples, however, are either grossly ignorant, very blind, or unpardonably forgetful, when they imagine that they have so thoroughly subjugated an independent mind, that it cannot think outside of them, nor see outside of their limit of vision. Every mind, when neither profitably, pleasantly nor honestly employed, is employed in directions to which these adverbs cannot be applied. You do not stop to think that theperson, whom you suppose embodies all your requirements, may possibly have a touch of self-pride still left, that will show itself when not overwhelmed by the majesty of your presence, and upon objects not mentioned in your well-selected list of requirements. It may be that when you think these are all met, she may be capable of others not set down, and and which she may not practice, except when from under vour direct surveillance.

Do you flatter yourselves that your wives, whom you have educated to suit you, devote all the time of your absence to the duties of family and home, especially when you are so very liberal as to supply them with nurses to take the children off their hands and servants for all work? Do you ever even think how their leisure time is employed, and for what purposes? In your overweening self-importance they find the very means of deceiving you. You think they are subjugated to you, while in reality they seek every possible opportunity to demonstrate to everybody else that they are perfectly free, and thus you are duped, while laboring under the very pleasing illusion that you have a veritable slave to your requirements. And these are the conditions you force upon those whom you make your wives, because, forsooth, they must be wives, lacking as they do the necessary accomplishments to be individuals.

Now we will, by your permission, gentlemen Temples, suggest that it would be far better for you in the end to possess yourselves of a little common sense, even if you are thereby obliged to part with a portion of your self-complacent importance; and also that you would permit those whom you make your companions to possess a little common sense of their own, if in some things it does not exactly fill your requirements. No certain happiness is possible in marriage unless two individuals meet, who, while being two distinct individuals, are so constituted as to be in their constitutions, naturally, the husband and the wife to each other. When this principle of marriage is practiced and admitted, and is acknowledged to be the real bond of marriage, in the place of the present required ceremony that now constitutes it, there will be fewer McFarland cases to disturb the harmony and shock the sensibilities of the truly refined of society. The legal requirements are perfectly proper and right, always supposing that the deeper and truer first exist. If these are lacking, were the legal bonds a thousand times stronger than they are, they would be constantly sundered by those whom they hold against their will.

No, Mr. Temple, if you would have good wives and true, you must permit them to be first good and true to themselves; you may then expect them to be so to you. True charity, as well as all other virtues and graces of mind and spirit, begin at home. And why should woman "eschew competition with man?" Does she become defiled thereby, or does she trespass upon some self-assumed right he has? And are you really the harder person and the rougher, because you habituate your counting-rooms? If so, it is time your wives should accompany you there. If not, why should they become so by going there with you? How can she be "one with you in all your pursuits;" how can she "sympathize with you in your difficulties," give you honest advice," if she is not practiced in the things that you "pursue," "have difficulty in," and require "advice" upon? Such shilly shally as this stuff and nonsense is, could only be born of a mind that regards woman as a thing, given to him simply for his own comfort and gratification, and not as his friend and ambitious equal, entitled to all the rights decreed her by character, ability and invlduality.

EQUALITY A NECESSITY.

THE SCHOOL OF DECEPTION—THE OBJECT OF FEMALE EDUCATION—
ITS HAPPY RESULTS—WHO ARE AT FAULT—SHALL SUCH PRAC-
TICES CONTINUE?

Women, as a general thing, are held by men in a state of semi-in-
dividuality. While they admit that, as personalities, they are different
from themselves, yet as determinate characters they propose to ignore
them, and to count them as but attachments to themselves. They contend that it takes two, a male and a female, to make a complete one,
reserving to themselves all the power of determining what these two in
one shall be. The female position being an utter negative in all that
goes to make up the external affairs of the world, it follows that women
bear about the same relation to the world, when compared with man,
that the moon does when compared with the sun, that is to say, they
shine when men will permit them.

We would not charge that men are entirely at fault for the unimportant position which women occupy in the world ; much of the error
is their own ; they are not all of them willing to take upon themselves
the burden of becoming individuals ; very many of them are content to
be simple automatons, to move only at the option of their controlling
master, to whom they have surrendered all self hood, to the full extent
of body and soul. It is to meet the requirements of this demand upon
them gracefully, becomingly, bewitchingly, that all their education is
modified and directed to.

Almost the first thing a girl is taught is, that she must not soil her
hands, nor spread her hands or feet, because that would make her ugly

in the eyes of men, whom it is made her first duty to study to please. All the way up from girlhood to maidenhood and to womanhood, the same kind of precept is constantly instilled into her receptive mind. All her studies are accomplishments rather than what can be reduced to use for practical ends. The single practical end girls are made acquainted with is how to catch a husband—who shall be the best "catch." Oh, the ignoble things that are instilled into the beautiful, fresh and innocent souls of our maidens! It is enough to make the angel world weep showers of tears. External adornments is placed so far above that of interior beauty and wealth that the mind and the soul are almost ignored.

Of what consequence is it to our modern belles whether they are truthful, honest and earnest, so that they are beautiful and accomplished? Their whole lives are devoted to falsifying their natural selves. From head to toe they are a living lie. When they lack hair, they overload their heads with that which is false to such an extent that they become hideous in the sight of the true devotee to nature and art. Art consists in making nature more beautiful, not in compelling contortions; and if the heaps of stuff worn by ladies to adorn their heads and to carry the idea to men that they are possessed of a magnificent quantity of hair, are not contortions or abortions of the designs of nature, we are at a loss to know what may be so designated. Next in order are their faces, which, lacking Nature's bloom of youth, they resort to " Laird's ;" but the attempt at deception is equally as apparent as in the case of the hair, and equally as destructive to the little natural beauty possessed as the resort to false hair is to the natural. Thus far the attempts at deception may be forgiven, for they are transparent frauds; but other practices that are resorted to are not thus entitled, because the extent of the deception practiced cannot be known so long as there is any necessity in its practice. And here the question naturally arises, For what purpose do ladies wear stuffed corsets? For what purpose do they pad their hips and calves, if it is not to appear more voluptuous and more enticing to the passions of men—which is the result produced? This is the effect, and they know it is the effect, and it can be for no other purpose that they practice it.

None can suppose that because a woman *appears* to be possessed of a beautifully developed form that that will make her intellectual acquirements or beauties of soul more prominent. On the contrary, such a person appeals directly to the animal instincts of the opposite sex. We would not have it understood that we deprecate physical beauty, but, on the contrary, we would have it distinctly accepted as one of the best gifts of God to the human family; and further would we distinctly assert that the highest degree of spiritual and intellectual beauty possible to be attained by human beings, is so possible only in that form which is the highest type of physical beauty.   What we do deprecate, and what we proclaim against, is the false pretence, the appearing to possess it when it is painfully lacking.   It is this deception so widely practiced that contributes one-half to the unhappiness of married life.   It has become so general that men are beginning to fear women when regarding the marriage state.   When they marry, they do not know whether they are marrying natural development or that which is basely artificial and deceptive, and they too often awake to find the latter to be the truth.

The case stands thus: Women dress to make themselves appear attractive to men; marriage with them is the one and only thing they are educated to; hence, this attractiveness with them has a first and second intention—first, to appear generally attractive to the other sex as a whole, and thereby to gain general admiration; second, that each woman may be able to be especially attractive to him whom she shall decide to allow the opportunity of wooing her.   By these artificial means she is assisted to win the man whom she consents to become attached to.   Thus far the matter progresses finely; but how about the sequel!   Those of you who have gained husbands thus must expect to lose them after the same fashion, by the charms of some other than yourselves; and we assert that you deserve to thus lose them, or to be subjected to some other righteous judgment.

It is scarcely to be wondered that so many men regard with a supreme contempt women who assert privileges beyond those included in a genuine wifely subjection.   They know that women generally are born, grow up, and are educated with the one idea of becoming the wife of somebody who shall be able to take care of her physical needs.   Why should they not affect and really feel disdain when some woman stands gloriously forth as independent and free—as entirely above depending upon anybody for anything; and competent to choose for herself whom she shall marry, or whether she will marry at all, and determined never to be *under the necessity of so doing* if her preferences shall decide otherwise.

Men may affect to think, and they may really think, they love a woman who is "moulded to their requirements;" but when they come in contact with one of nature's noblewomen, an admiration will be drawn from them which they cannot control, and which is, as a general thing, utterly destructive to any attachment previously possessed for the "pretty woman," who bows in wifely submission to her husband's supreme control

We, therefore, contend that there can be no true and securely lasting and natural attachment between the sexes in the marriage state that is not based in truth, in nature and in perfect equality of condition previous to its being entered upon. The sooner women awake to the consciousness of the truth about this matter of false pretences, and come to the resolution to stand or fall upon their true merits or demerits, so much the sooner will they cease to enter upon miserable and unprofitable lives. If you would be wise, be true to yourselves and speak truth to man with both your tongue and form. To deceive with the latter is as much a lie as to speak untruth with the former.

ARE WOMEN INDIVIDUALS, OR ARE THEY PERSONAL NONENTITIES?

CONDITION OF WOMEN UNDER THE DIFFERENT FORMS OF GOVERN-
MENT, POLITICALLY, SOCIALLY, INTELLECTUALLY—INEQUALITY
MEANS INFERIORITY—THE INCONSIDERATENESS OF WOMEN—INDI-
VIDUALITY FOR ALL.

In surveying the situation occupied by woman, it is not surprising
that this query should arise in the minds of those who observe realities
rather than the glittering appearances, by which things are often shrouded
by those who desire that realities should not become apparent. We
do not believe that many women realize the whole truth regarding
themselves. Aside from a certain degree of moral power possessed in
some quarters, there never were representatives of humanity more completely subjugated than are the women of countries that profess to be
republican. They are in precisely the same condition of those men
who, by some overt act, have lost their citizenship. We challenge you
who say us nay to show that this is not the case. In countries despotic
and monarchical there is not that vast difference of condition between
the sexes that exists in republics. Women there come nearer possessing an equality of political power, as it is not under all constitutional
and limited monarchies that all men have a political voice.

Under other forms of government the women are still more nearly
equal, for in many countries voting is unknown. Do women ever stop
to consider that under republican forms of government, as distinguished
from monarchies, the privileges of men generally are vastly augmented
and those of women remain unchanged? Do they always desire to re-

main in this dormant condition regarding their privileges? It is not merely political privileges that women voluntarily forego. In the domain of commerce and finance they have, like the serfs of Russia, to some extent, made inroads; but these exceptional cases are those where women have been obliged to resort to them, because thrown upon their own resources; or because they have had no master to determine for them that they should not take such steps. Intellectually, also, women have exhibited some brilliant examples of individuality; so, too, have they done in all ages; but here even they lack that positive power which always proceeds from a consciousness of superiority of condition. Socially, the instances of individuality are always those of ignominy, and the individuals are made a curse and blight of society. They do not receive the consideration of " neighbors " at their hands.

But for all these inequalities there is a prime inequality which conduces directly to them, and this is political inequality, or the absence of the female element in the control of those things upon which all others hinge, and by which all others, to a very considerable extent, are determined. Political inequality is a direct admission of inferiority on the part of those subjected to it, and a direct assertion of inferiority on the part of those who prohibit equality. All inequalities are the direct result of a lack of individuality, and a lack of individuality is the result of our system of educating the young.

To become individualized presupposes being independent, self-reliant and self-supporting. This is individuality. All individuals, therefore, must have a direct interest in the rules and regulations under which they shall be compelled to be self-reliant. While women depend upon men to provide for all their pecuniary interests, individuality is a thing of little importance, and those women who have never known what it is to earn the supply of their daily wants, can well say that they forego political equality, and consider every woman who demands it as "strong-minded " and almost masculine. But let revolution come; let these dependent women be thrown upon their own resources, and their convictions would soon change. They would not only demand that legislation should be somewhat in their interests, but they would also demand an equal right to form a part of legislation.

We would ask, then, what is the objection to extending the political rights possessed by man to such women as are similarly conditioned to men; to those who are independent and who have an equal interest with man in the laws under the operations of which they must provide for themselves.

If Congress deny to women generally the privilege of suffrage, upon the plea that women generally are averse to it, let them grant it to women who demand it, and whose conditions warrant the demand being made. Place women upon the same footing with men, when they occupy similar positions, and are similarly conditioned. Surely this measure of justice cannot be denied by the most conservative men, nor ridiculed by the most "sensible" feminine women, unless, forsooth, there is a determination on the part of men to hold women in continuous vassalage, and on the part of the majority of women to willingly submit to being vassals.

There is, however, one tendency in the human family which neither "conservative" men nor "feminine" women can prevent, by any of their fondness for old customs and things—that is, Individuality; and it is this characteristic in women, as well as in men, that will not only demand, but obtain all the common privileges for themselves that are enjoyed by any individuals under the same government. Suffrage may be denied a little longer to women who demand it, but equality, as applied to both sexes, must and will obtain in all departments of life; in those of duty as in those of privilege.

IMPORTANCE OF THE WOMEN QUESTION.

A QUESTION OF HUMANITY—FEAR OF THE TRUTH DAPARTING—
STRONG-MINDED WOMEN'AND WEAK-MINDED MEN—SUFFRAGE ONLY
THE BEGINNING OF THE MOVEMENT—THE ULTIMATE PERFECTION
OF THE RACE DEPENDENT UPON THE FREEDOM OF WOMEN AND
HER INDIVIDUAL RIGHT TO HERSELF—FALSE PRETENCES OF THE
OPPONENTS OF SUFFRAGE — THEY UNDERSTAND THE REAL QUES-
TION AT ISSUE—THE POSITIONS OF THE SEXES IN THEIR RELA-
TIONS TO EACH OTHER TO BE TRANSPOSED.

There is no single question which is agitating the public mind that possesses the magnitude and the importance of the so-called "Woman Question." We cannot coincide in the appropriateness of this title; instead of being thus called, it should much more properly be called THE QUESTION OF HUMANITY. It has heretofore been very generally overlooked that woman has fully as great responsibilities to perform, and those that have fully as great influence upon humanity as man. It is beginning to be possible for the very few who appreciate this fact to be heard, without receiving the slush of all the opprobrious epithets a filthy world has at its command to daub with.

Until quite recently, it was sufficient to condemn a woman to know that she was "strong-minded," and equally sufficient to damn a man, to know that he was weak-minded enough to sympathize with such strong-mindedness, not to go so far as to advocate it. It is astonishing to see how much better people understand, appreciate and adopt *truths*, when they are presented by those who occupy an *unquestionable* position

in society. So evident is this sometimes, that it has very much the
appearance that it is the person and not the truth which is adopted. Still,
when we take a more comprehensive view of mankind, we have reason
for a better hope for individuals, and that each will weigh, and discard
or accept, whatever is presented them, upon its merits, and their conception óf them, without regard to the channel through which it shall
come.

That the Woman Question is the question of humanity may be a
somewhat new and novel idea to many, if not to most, minds. To con
sider it as such, however, raises it far above the simple question of suffrage; indeed, suffrage is that portion of it that shall open up the real
question for consideration, and not only open it, but will force all others
into being considered. And it is this undefined portion of the involve-
ment that brings down upon the cause such general and sweeping denunciation from that portion of men who are constitutionally predis-
posed to advancement, and to the extension of liberty and equality to
those over whom they have control. We have heretofore shown that
the women of this country are possessed of less proportionate rights
and privileges than those of any country not republican : that is to say,
that while the men have greatly advanced their own privileges, they
have assumed for themselves the same position occupied by the despots
of the world—that of determining the condition of all those under
them. Women have remained stationary. It practically amounts to
to this, and to nothing less.

It may be said that women now have vast power and influence.
Granted, in individual cases; but they would still remain possessed of
this power and influence were their further natural rights and privileges
extended them, whereby they would become still more potent. Nor can
this fuss about the moral power of the sex much longer divert its attention from the fact that it is despoiled of all material power. The acquisition of political power cannot be construed to mean loss of moral
or social power, or purity. If this is an argument against female suffrage, it is equally a plausible one against male suffrage. This hum-
buggery about the distinctions of sex in political considerations has
lasted just about long enough. If suffrage is good for men, it is also
good for women, upon the same rule ; and if it is the part of despot-
ism to deny men the right of governing themselves, and if they that
do so deny them, are despots and tyrants, so, too, are they who deny to
women the right to govern themselves despots and tyrants, upon the
same rule. When the Congress of the United States refuses to extend

the privilege of suffrage to women when asked for it, they are only re-enacting the part played by those who desired to hold our forefathers in subjection by the same withholding of privilege.

But, as we have said, this part of the Woman Question is simply the entering-wedge that shall open the more important parts of it. Upon women, as the mothers of society, devolve the great task of perfecting the race. If the millennium ever come—and we have the most perfect faith that it will—it must come through the mothers of humanity. Millennium presupposes humanity arrived at such a degree of development as to admit of the operation of perfect laws, based on those principles that will apply during all times, to all people, in all nations. So long as women are the mere slaves of men, forced by the laws of marriage to submit their bodies to them, whenever and wherever they may so determine, and by thus being subjected are still further and more barbarously forced to become the unwilling mothers of unwished-for children, so long will the millennium days be delayed. In other words, so long as women are forced to prostitute themselves by law, just so long will the sex remain in a degraded and undeveloped condition, and be utterly incapable of producing children of healthy minds and bodies.

The mothers of humanity are treated in the matter of maternity more like brutes than humans; while the mothers of brutes are treated more like human beings than brutes. The offspring of brutes are the subjects of much greater consideration, in all senses of the term, than the offspring of humanity are; and it is just here and nowhere else, that the main part of the Woman Question begins, for it is here that the perfecting process of the race must begin, and therefore this is the real point at issue. As we said, it is the undefined consciousness of this in the hearts of men that causes them to treat the initiatory step of suffrage with such affected contempt; they do not care so much for what the future of humanity may be, as they do for the retention of the power they now possess over women.

It is all bosh and nonsense for men to continue the delusion, that to introduce women into politics is to debase her. If politics are really so damned and debased as to corrupt all who have anything to do with them, it is quite time that it should be so known, and quite time that women should force themselves into politics, for the purpose of exposing their actual condition. We are perfectly aware of the festering and rotten conditions that exist, and that the process of sloughing must soon begin; we know that money is the power that controls the suf-

frage of many men at all elections, and, for this special reason, we desire the suffrages of women whom money will not buy.

The positions assumed by men in denying suffrage to women are
the advanced redoubts, guarding the way to and protecting the main
citadel, which they desire to remain wholly in their control; these once
gained, they know that the citadel is no longer safe; while we protest
that the gaining of the outer works are merely for the purpose of making sure of the surrender of the citadel within, the command of which,
women are determined upon having, as a matter of right and justice
to the sex.

The Woman Question, then, rises high above the simple question
of political privilege to that of what shall determine the future condition of the race; hence the suffrage privilege is regarded by those who
comprehend it, as was before stated, simply as the entering-wedge, that
shall open the main questions, and reveal their real and general importance, not simply to women as a sex, but to humanity as a whole.
When women who have heretofore refrained from the woman movement shall be brought to this understanding, they will no longer remain
in the passive and acquiescent state they now occupy. Being conscious
of their real importance to the future of the world, they will gain just
so much the more dignity, as that position presupposes over that they
now occupy, as the simple attachments to men. Men under the new
regime will become the companions of women instead, and will receive
it as a special favor if so permitted to be. And this is the ultimate of
the Woman Question.

THE RAPID SPREAD OF THE WOMAN QUESTION.

ITS EXTENT UNAPPRECIATED—EVIDENCES—THE LEAVEN THAT IS
LEAVENING THE WHOLE LUMP—PRACTICAL DEMONSTRATION—THE
NEXT GENERAL ELECTIONS—WOMAN'S DUTY—ONE MILLION WO-
MEN TO DEMAND POLITICAL EQUALITY FROM CONGRESS—WILL
CONGRESS IGNORE THEM—ARE WOMEN IN EARNEST?

Very few people comprehend the real extent of the Woman Question. It is very young in years still, but its strength and growth are
not to be measured by its age; that must be judged from other rules.
It is, however, true, that for a long time after the question was mooted
as one that was to agitate the sentiment of the country, it made but
little perceptible progress. There were but a few brave persons who
would proclaim what they conceived to be the right and the justice of
the points involved. A very great number of persons, who received
the new doctrine, harbored it secretly in their minds against the time
they were confident it could and would be broadly proclaimed, and in
being so would not necessarily injure the reputation of its advocates,
nor commit them to the ban of society as dangerous members of it.
    One of the best evidences that the time draws near when justice
shall know no distinctions of sex is, that where once obloquy attached
to the advocacy of "the question" the deepest respect is now commanded from all, by its earnest advocates. There are but a very
few of the best newspapers that attempt to burlesque it any longer;
they treat it as one of the open questions of the day, which, for such

5

constitutional devotees to the popular side of all new questions as they are, is wonderfully refreshing. Even the unreasonable dogmatism of some of the so-called Christians is becoming "leavened," and the signs are promising and numerous, that the little "leaven" years ago added to the lump of humanity is rapidly progressing in its work, throughout all its strata and ramifications.

Certain it is, that, where five years ago *one paper in a hundred* only, contained something about the progress of the Woman Question, now only *one in a hundred* can be found that has not a very considerable space devoted to it; and this has only become true to this extent within the present year. This fact is attributable to a variety of causes, but specially to two causes.

Since the settlement of the slavery question and the virtual reconstruction of the country, the radical sentiment of the country that before expended itself in that direction, has found vent upon this question, which is the next great question of universal justice that comes up for consideration and adjustment.

Again, it was not until quite recently that women made any practical application of what had been previously asserted, that they were competent to do whatever man could do, subject only to the limitations of nature, function and constitution. Since women first began to show their capacity for individuality, they have done it in such faint and unobtrusive ways that no impression was made by it upon the public mind. The result of all their dress-making, fancy store-keeping, school, teaching, &c., &c., did not amount to sufficient moral force to carry any considerable weight of conviction home to the hearts of practical men.

But now that women boldly advance into the heat and strife of active business life, and show themselves competent to compete with the shrewdest and most experienced men, and also show an administrative capacity equal to all emergencies in all directions, the heretofore matter-of-fact business men begin to open their eyes in amazement and astonishment. Some have already recovered sufficiently from this condition, to question, whether they have not been doing themselves as well as women an irreparable wrong, by denying them the rights and privileges of a perfect equality. Some even exclaim in the most extravagant terms of admiration regarding capacity, when exhibited by woman, and with the utmost readiness and gallantry withdraw all opposition, saying it is not for me to say any longer what shall be the limits "that woman" shall be confined to.

Talk, fuss and confusion, which is pretty nearly the amount of progress attained by the majority of women advocates, was all very well, and led the way to what should follow; but it required representatives, who could do something more than this, and those who have demonstrated the practical side of the Woman Question are the ones that have wrought the recent remarkable change in the treatment of the subject, at the hands of the press and public generally. In other words, one ounce of practice has done more than all theoretical teaching, though the teaching necessarily preceded the practice.

Even the demonstration that women are equal to the severest tests of business was not sufficient to accomplish all this, but when it was also demonstrated that women, politically, philosophically and scientifically, could be, and were, the equals of men, which capacities were deemed entirely lacking in the sex, then the last possible objection was removed, and the sex in reality was lifted at once into the realm of possibilities common with man.

What is now the practical lesson of this result? It is this: that every woman should mark out for herself some distinct course to pursue, which shall not only be an exemplification of her individual rights and capabilities, but also her contribution to the sum total of efforts and possibilities of the sex. Women will never be lifted from their present positions of inferiority by man; they must rise from them themselves, and boldly—defiantly if need be—advance, capture and maintain positions of equality. If the capacity to do this is once seen, men will not stand in your way long. If they do they will not be able to resist the general uprising the present decade will witness.

In the coming elections the women should be in the field, and for all important offices should have their candidates, and should advocate their election by all possible means. This will, at least, convince those, still stubborn, that we are in earnest, which would be a good way toward ultimate victory. We need not fear that the small results will injure the cause. The Abolition party, which grew into the grand, mighty and magnificent Republican party, was once so small that it numbered but one advocate. In twenty years that one advocate made it the mightiest power that has yet existed on the face of the Western Hemisphere. If such results grew from so small a beginning in so short a space of time, what may we not expect for the woman movement in this still later and more rapidly progressive day!

After the next general State elections in the country, let it be possible for us to show to the Congress of the United States that there are

1,000,000 earnest and untiring women demanding the right and privilege of suffrage. Then let Congress ignore the question if it dare. This is eminently a practical age, and men require demonstration. This once obtained, the adoption of the thing demonstrated is only a question of time. Women have been most persistently impractical, and for this reason : the claims of the few who have been bold enough to make them, for an equalty in all things with man, have been laughed at, as having been made in jest. Let it be no longer possible for this shaft to be hurled against us. Let us convince all men that we are fear fully in earnest, and, if it need be, do this in a quarter that will bring them to a perception and consciousness that we mean it. We have the power ; let it no longer be wasted in obtaining *favor*, but applied in demanding *equality*—first, from *gallantry;* second, as of *right,* when gallantry fails. Thousands of women know their power ; let these same thousands use it for different purposes, and for the benefit of a suffering humanity, in unloosing the chains that bind woman, and thus make her, individually, her own free self.

ONE OF THE MAIN ISSUES OF THE COMING CANVASS.

OLD PARTIES WITH NEW ISSUES — PRINCIPLE THE INSPIRATION OF ALL PARTIES — WHICH PARTY SHALL CHAMPION EQUALITY FOR WOMEN?—THE QUESTION CANNOT BE IGNORED—IT MUST BE MET AND SETTLED.

It is getting to be pretty generally conceded by the best judges of political tendencies, that all the special issues that have divided political parties during the past few years are now dead, and that the parties representative of them are defunct. All the various general questions of finance, revenue, tariff and general home and foreign policies, form no dividing lines; they are held *pro* and *con*, promiscuously, by both Democrats and Republicans. All the leading questions that developed the Republican party, and upon which the war was fought, are forever disposed of, while the Democratic party that was its opponent was composed quite as much from the old Whig party as from the Democratic party that existed previously.

It will be seen, then, that though the same terms or names remain, the individuals that form the component parts of the parties are continually changing; thus, those who were once Whigs have since been Democrats, while those who are Republicans were once both Democrats and Whigs. It is quite possible that the names Democrat and Republican may extend into future politics, but it is still more certain that they will never be represented by the same persons nor representative of the same issues. It is more probable, however, that one of these party names will disappear as the Whig did, and its members be distributed among the remaining and the new.

When the Republican party based itself upon the Slavery Question, that question was fully as unpopular as the Woman Question now is, nevertheless it flourished upon it, and attained a power and influence never attained by any previous party. The Woman Question will be one of the principal questions that will divide the general mind previous to the close of the next Presidential canvass, and will be adopted by one or the other of the parties that contests that election. It would not be wise nor politic for the citizens of the United States who are entitled to suffrage, to form a party upon the distinct issue of female suffrage. The real strength of such a party could not be made felt, and such efforts would be wasted; but they who are favorable to such suffrage being extended, must become incorporated with a party, and thereby shape its movements favorably to it. It properly belongs with the new labor party, and the question is more likely to find general favor there than in either the Democratic or Republican parties, providing they should both survive.

When it comes that one of the great political parties becomes the advocate of female equality, the other will naturally be opposed to it; then, and not till then, will it be known how diffusively the question has taken root in the popular mind. Never having been in position to divide the sympathies of the people, there have been no means of knowing their real sentiment. Besides, when even an unpopular question is brought prominently before the public, if based in justice it will constantly gain strength by being agitated. Thus, before the South attempted to compel the North into acceptance of their theory of States Rights regarding slavery, very many who were at heart opposed to the principle of slavery, had never taken sides, and never would have, so long as the South remained satisfied with what it had; the moment that they desired slavery to become virtually national, the whole people sided either for or against it, and thus precipitated the dread issue that followed.

If negro slavery were wrong in principle and altogether behind the age, how much more so should present female inequalities be considered—surely you would not deny woman a privilege you have extended to the negro? The growing requirements of women to be able to be independent, self-reliant and self-supporting, make it an absolute necessity for her to have her influence over the legislation that is to govern the circumstances under which she must be so. It is this plain statement of the case that makes it evident to all thoughtful and sensible men, that women must know what they desire better than they do or can for them. Even if men were to grant women all the legislation in her behalf that she herself would enact were she admitted to legislation, that would not suffice. No man would like to surrender his right to suffrage, even if he knew legislation would be just the same. It is not a question, in the first instance, of benefit; it is a simple question of right; and if it is good for men to vote, why should it not be better for women, who have more need of special protection in the time coming, when she is to be thrown more and more upon herself, in all things regarding life, liberty and happiness?

This being, then, a question of principle that has been raised, it will never be possible to crush it out; it will continue to spread and to attract attention until the principle is acceded to on the part of those who now are either opposed or indifferent to it.

The Negro Question vitalized the Republican Party, because there was a principle involved in it; so, too, will the Woman Question vitalize the party that shall become its champion. If the Republican party did a great service to the cause of general civilization, the party that shall lift the banner of female freedom and equality will do it a much greater service. Negro slavery involved a few millions of individuals. The Woman Question involves hundreds of millions scattered all over the face of the earth. It is meet that the country which was almost the last to abjure slavery should be the first to enfranchise woman. We lost much prestige by clinging to slavery; let us gain what we lost by boldly meeting and settling this newer, greater and graver question, which other nations have scarcely begun to talk about; that they have not is not strange, for there is not the degree of inequality attaching to woman in other countries that there is here.

This question will be forced upon the attention of our next Congress, and by being so will grow into one of immense importance to the parties that shall contest future elections, if it does not in fact become the question upon which they will hinge.

THE SIXTEENTH AMENDMENT.

ITS NECESSITY TO AROUSE WOMEN TO AN APPRECIATION OF THEM-
SELVES—FEMALE APATHY—ALL MOVEMENT, PROGRESS—THE APPLE
OF EDEN—WOMAN'S AMBITION—WOMAN'S CONDITION ANALYZED—
FREEDOM FOR WOMEN AS WELL AS FOR MEN—THE TRUE PRINCI-
PLE BEHIND THE SCENES—SUFFRAGE FIRST—INDEPENDENCE NEXT
FREEDOM NEXT—NATURE OUR BEST TEACHER.

Nothing is more astonishing to one who has gained her freedom
than to regard the utter apathy with which women in general accept
their condition. "Where ignorance is bliss 'tis folly to be wise,"
seems of almost universal application to the relations sustained by
women to the world at large. Either this is so, or otherwise they,
"having eyes see not, and having ears hear not," what immediately
concerns their salvation. Salvation has but one signification to the
people of earth since the explosion of the doctrine of a local hell of
fire and brimstone which is paved with infants' skulls.

Salvation to man is just what growth—evolution—is to all the
departments of the universe; it is going from lower to higher conditions, or, strictly speaking, making a progress from one condition into
and through new conditions, each one of which produces growth.
Movement is progress and progress is growth; a condition once experienced can never be retrograded; it is an acquisition ; and in this view
of the subject all movements are progressive, whether the acquisition
seem beneficial or deleterious for the time. "No punishment for the
present seemeth joyous but grievous, but afterward it yieldeth the
peaceable fruits of righteousness." Thus it is with all acquisition of

experience, whether that experience for the time seemeth "joyous" or "grievous;" and this is the philosophy of life; the science of growth; the religion of all nature.

While all nature bustles and hurries to improve its conditions and to change its relations, woman, specifically as woman, remains indifferent, apathetic and fixed; while all the human capacities are rapidly enlarging; while the human mind is constantly becoming broader and deeper, and capable of greater, sublimer, diviner things, woman rests content within her circumscribed limits of action. "Thus far shalt thou go and no further," seems to her a line over whose limits she dare not break, lest the beyond shall lead to forbidden fruits, whose tasting shall as really damn man, as the eating of the apple by Eve has symbolically damned the race to this day. Under this accusation about the apple, woman rests, with all the patience that could possibly belong to a conviction of its justice; through the absurdity of the narration as having actually occurred has been completely shown by the keen analysis of science, still the effects of its having so long been taught as fact, hang like a pall over the brightest hopes of the mothers of humanity.

The doctrine that woman was created for man still holds the dominant position in the world's mind; this is strictly true, but not more so than that man was created for woman; nor more so than that all things were created for each other. This intimate system of relationship extends from the simplest forms of organic life upward, and when thoroughly understood, teaches the great lesson of life, to wit: that we are, because all things have been; and that nothing within the realm of the whole earth can be so isolated as not to bear relations to every other thing in it. These great general truths are gradually dawning upon the minds of men, and are every day making the position that woman has resigned herself to, more and more to be deprecated.

Taking woman as a unit, what are her aspirations? to what are her thoughts and hopes directed? what purposes has she in her soul to live to work out? From the cradle to the grave it is but one thing; the substance of which is to captivate man. For this she is born, reared, educated and moulded; for this she lives; for it she dies. Were the possibilities which might grow out of this taken at all into the consideration, there might be some wisdom even in this; were the probabilities that are very certain to grow out of this even considered, there would be great wisdom exhibited; but neither the one nor the other enters into "the means and schemes" in one case in a thousand.

How many that enter the marriage state know absolutely anything either practically or theoretically about the duties and responsibilities that they are to incur? The one thought is to get well married off; that accomplished, life, which should then just begin, in fact comes to its real end; they can no longer be said to retain their individuality; what they may have exhibited previously, then becomes either merged into the man she has sworn to obey, or is by him first modified, next controlled, and then subdued. Some may question these assertions, but let any woman ask herself if she can do what her own inclinations prompt her to, and she will find she must either answer that she cannot, or that she is inclined to do just what will please her lord and master, and nothing beyond. Now, what is wanting in the relations of the sexes is, the power on the part of both to be themselves, while at the same time they are harmoniously united; that is, that each has the first and best right to himself or herself and all opinions, and that in possessing them and acting upon them, no cause of dissatisfaction or even of unpleasantness to the other should arise therefrom. Marriage, as practiced, simply means subjugation and support for the wife; the right to command and demand for the husband. In this relation, when the very first requisite should be equality of right and interest, that of woman is completely submerged by the force of the contract, supported and made possible by the custom and the long practice of society under the intolerent rule of Mrs. Grundy.

Behind all these false conditions, customs and their results, and in the very heart and core of society, is practiced a very great deal of the true principle of freedom; but this is done in a way that shuts the eye of the public and its self-constituted censors. One of the first needs of society is to be able to do openly what it already does secretly; every person needs the moral courage to do whatever his soul tells him he should do, openly and before the world, neither courting its notice nor dreading it. With the full assurance and approval of their own consciences, everybody should become their own law-givers; and common decency and respect for self should stop the universal question: If I do this that my soul tells me I should, what will people say? This is the slavery society needs freedom from. Every member of society should be so full of their own rights and desire to act them, that they could find no time to busy themselves about others' pursuit of the same.

The possibility for woman to assert this right to self-government and to self-control, depends upon one thing which lies at the very basis of all movements in this direction, and that is the capacity to be independent. The whole tenor of the education of women must change; she must be educated to know that she is an individual, liable at all times to be compelled to take sole care of herself. The immediate result of such a course would be to make her still more attractive to man, to whom she would not be obliged to surrender herself to become his mere slave, for that is the only word that expresses the truth of the condition.

The difficulty every one encounters who enters upon the advocacy of more and better freedom for woman is, that "Free love" is at the bottom of it. That is just what we would have said : for if to advocate freedom is "free love" as contra indicated from *forced love*, then by all means do we accept the application. If there is one foul, damning blot upon woman's nature and capacities, it is this system that compels her to manifest and act a love that is forced; this kind of love is all the prostitution there is in the world. None of the acts that may be suggested by a genuine love can be held to be the prostitution of the power or capacity exhibited.

It is unfortunate that terms should have such sweeping application, and in reality so little real meaning, and still be so freely used by those who know not what they are saying. All the natural attractions nature has within herself, are representatives of the principle of free love; and it is quite time the bugaboo that connects itself with this term should be exploded ; and quite time that people should call things by their right names. And just at this point we declare as a principle and rule of action, that whatever lessons nature, in all her most beautiful variety and modes of action, teaches, it is quite safe for humanity to pattern after. Nature is our best and only authoritative teacher. If we look to or accept other than her laws, we shall be under the necessity, sooner or later, of revolting, to free ourselves from the voluntary bondage we place ourselves under. Yet nature even has her grades of beauty and development; but they all proceed by the same general law; the lower and the higher exemplify by their action the real degree of ascent they have attained, and in freedom of expression there is no cause of censure but simply of comparison to determine that degree.

In this question of woman's condition that must necessarily occupy the public mind, until a solution is arrived at, a grand advance would be made toward a solution, could everybody be freed from the slavery imposed by superstition, tradition, ignorance and authority. All these are so many blocks in the way of progress, and are firmly held by those whom the ages have to drag along. Those who are desirous of remaining the willing subjects of such slavery have the undoubted right to do so ; but we protest against the right of those who desire it, to force others who do not, to submit themselves to its rule. What every woman wants who has arrived at a just perception of her powers, capacities, possibilities, rights and should-be privileges is, the freedom to avail herself of them, to her own use and benefit, and not to their use and benefit as expounded and understood by others interested in their withholding.

The necessity of the Sixteenth Amendment to enable woman as a sex to come into possession and control of herself, must be evident to all reasoning minds; she now is in the possession and control of man, and must and does submit to all his domination ; though some may at times rebel against the too severe administration of this privilege of control, the privilege remains, and all women are subjected to it, because there is no authority to which she can appeal. The privilege of the ballot will open the direct way to individuality and independence, and these will prepare women for freedom; freedom will give opportunity for the outworkings of woman's better nature and instincts, and in these the regeneration of the race will be a possibility.

As has been before stated, the Woman Question is not merely one of suffrage, but one of humanity, to which suffrage will open the direct way ; and as such it is the most important question that agitates the public mind, and one that cannot, must not, will not, shall not be ignored.

WOMAN'S DUTIES.

"Charity begins at home," is an axiom that has been acknowledged by the great and good of all ages and climes. Even in semi-barbarous times, the signification was of considerable force; but as centuries have rolled away, its pertinence has become with each of them more explicit and sharply defined. Rendered in different language, and applied specially to humanity, it would mean that whatever it is good for a person to render to others, should first be rendered to him or herself. In fact, a person cannot be just to others unless self-justice lie at the foundation of it.

Viewing the Woman Question from this standpoint, what are the aspects it presents to the present for its consideration and solution? In the first instance, woman must first be true to herself before she can be true in any sense to man. The possibility of woman being true to her own nature depends wholly upon her capacity and her right to freedom of choice in all things that relate specifically to her as woman.

We examine the course society and its customs have laid down for her to follow, and vainly endeavor to find the first instance wherein woman has positive, determining power. She is born, and in childhood is nurtured, and in youth is educated, not for herself, but for man; this process completed, she is then bound, soul and body, to him, by bonds which, prove they never so obnoxious, she may not be released from except after having performed some atrocity of which the law can take advantage to forever after put a blight upon her. Whatever aspirations she may have, whatever ambitions may have birth within her soul, whatever intuitions may spring from her warm, generous-natured heart, they are each and all circumscribed by this formula of growth, which has been so rigorously insisted upon.

The first duty, then, that woman owes herself is, to demand for herself her right to freedom, without which there can be no individual responsibility. Government existing everywhere, gives to its respective subjects its different degrees of freedom, ranging from that in which the voice of one man is the law of the country to that of republican-ism, in which the voice of all men is the law of the land. The only difference between an absolute monarchy and republicanism, so far as they apply to woman, is, that the first is the " one-man " power, while the last is the " many-men " power, in both of which woman is as com-plete a subject, without power or the right to appeal from power, as man is under the absolute monarch.

Woman, then, under a republican government, is under an abso lute monarchy. It does not matter that there may be—that there is— a difference in the kind of power exercised, or in the stringency of the laws that were and are in force—the principle is the same. What kind of freedom is it that a people has by sufferance, compared with that en-joyed by right? In this question there is contained all the advantage there is to be gained by self-government. There have been monarchs in the past under whom the people enjoyed as much freedom and equal-ity as woman does under the republic. If she have any power in or over government, it is obtained by her personal power as woman over man; this same power has been possessed and exercised in all ages and nations. There is, then, no difference in principle between the absolute government now exercised over woman and that which was exercised over the whole people ages since. From that power and rule man has freed himself, but his sisters still linger under its baneful influence— baneful, because it militates against her obtaining individuality.

When woman obtains the same kind of freedom and exercises the same rights that man does, she will begin to live for the same ends that man does. At present marriage is the all in all for woman. It is the end of woman's individual existence, instead of being, as it should be, a means to a still greater and more glorious consummation. Whatever greatness man has ever attained, has been gained by the exercise of his individual powers; his adapting his acquirements to some grand practical and general result. Had there been some lesser object for him to generally consider the end of attainment, there would have been much less of progress for the world. Now, woman is naturally more intuitive—perceptive—than man, and therefore a better perceiver of the real requirements of the ages than he is or can be. She would be, under equal circumstances, more inventive than he, while he would be better adapted to working out her inventions.

It would be an instructive lesson were all the great attainments made by woman analyzed, to find which were made by her as the woman, and which by her as the wife. It has been the free women who have been great, or those who, by nature, could not be subjugated, even by the marriage contract. It is proverbial that husbands do not wish their wives to become conspicuous, even by great actions. They wish to ever remain the "I am." Greatness brings honor and homage, which men cannot endure to see paid by others to their wives. In this practice they deny that they have confidence in their wives. When wives are brought into active contact with the world, it has been, and still is, to a great extent, the rule to consider her as "abandoned." In fact, men make it their special duty to attempt to stigmatize all women who move outside of the specific circle of the wife as "common women." If they were to be judged by the same rule, it is much to be feared they would generally be found just what they endeavor to make it seem that women are.

It is this difference in the rule of judgment that obtains between man and woman that must be eradicated. One law for him and another for her cannot be much longer exercised. It is not that woman, in demanding freedom, desires it that she may make use of it in the same directions man does his freedom. With her delicate sensibilities and warm-natured, devoted soul, absence makes those whom she loves still "more" to her. It is not within her to be dissolute when not under the personal influence of home. No man is willing to allow his wife the same privileges he makes use of when away from home. Look to the numerous houses of prostitution in all large cities; they are supported by men whose wives are at home performing their duties and maintaining their loyalty as wives. . The knowledge of the extent of these practices is fast diffusing itself among wives, and if it obtain firm hold in their hearts, man may not expect them to remain loyal while they are disloyal. If it is such a luxury—such a relief—for husbands to play truant, why should not wives imitate their well-set and long-maintained example? Do many husbands dream how much they already do?

But this is not the direction freedom moves in. All legitimate liberty and equality which is guaranteed by a government leads to virtuous practices, and all illegitimate freedom obtained in spite of law and order leads directly in the reverse direction; and this is the philosophy of government. Greater freedom is always followed by more virtue; thus it has been in all stages of government, and thus it will remain so long as government exists.

Woman's duty to herself is thus, first, to demand and obtain the same freedom, the same equality, the same rights to privileges that man has. This gained, there are other duties that will legitimately follow from it, such as the duties of individuality in education, practice and support.

To man she owes the duties of the sister and the wife, in just the same proportionate measure that man owes her the duties of brother and husband. This and no more. First, she *must* be HERSELF; being this *well*, she is competent to be the good sister and the devoted wife, which means a great deal more than to be the wife custom now exacts of her. It means to be so from principle. A person who thinks in his heart that he will perform such and such things, and yet has not the personal courage to carry them out, is no less the thief or murderer at heart; all such persons are in just as much need of regeneration as those are who carry out their thoughts and plans.

Virtue, in the common acceptance of that phrase, should be judged by the same rule. If a man is honest because the law compels him to be, it is no virtue that he possesses that can claim the reward. Honesty for the sake of honesty—from principle rooted in the heart—is what constitutes virtue; so, too, is loyalty between husband and wife to be· adjudged. It then appears by this rule, that if husbands and wives are loyal only because law and custom compel them to be so, there is no virtue in such loyalty; and, consequently, that there would be just as much real loyalty were there no restricting power. Devotion to truth, right and high morality, then, is only to be gained by greater apparent freedom—and this it is the duty of woman to obtain.

SUFFRAGE AND MARRIAGE.

THE SIXTEENTH AMENDMENT; ITS RELATION TO MARRIAGE — FREE-
DOM TO WOMAN MEANS THE PURIFICATION OF ALL THE RELATIONS
OF THE SEXES—THOSE WHO THROW DIRT SHOW THEIR OWN FILTHI-
NESS—OUR OWN POSITION DEFINED SO THAT FOOLS, EVEN, MAY
COMPREHEND IT.

There has been very much written and said regarding marriage, in connection with its relations to the question of suffrage. With this as with all imperfectly understood (imperfectly understood, because not yet demonstrated by facts) questions, very crude, antagonistic and un-philosophic positions are assumed by both its advocates and its oppo-sers. It is one of those questions which, above almost all others, most nearly affect the basis of society, and should, therefore, be dis-cussed with the utmost calmness, deliberation and sound sense, and whoever attempts discussion, whether by mouth or pen, should divest themselves of every prejudice that custom may have endowed them with, so that the actual conditions may appear without embellishments of any kind or color. The processes of demonstrated science should teach the manner of treatment which should be practiced in all inves-tigation. They say that if it is attempted to make the desired results to conform to the laws of custom, or the authorities of prejudice, the investigation might just as well be discontinued until a clear field is opened.

Very much, if not the most, of opposition the suffrage movement encounters, is raised because it is supposed that its success will in some unaccountable and inexplicable manner interfere with the relations of the sexes; in other words, with marriage. If there is one absurdity more completely absurd than all other absurdities, it is the supposition that anything, anywhere, raised by anybody, can ever abolish marriage;

6

and we make this assertion with all the emphasis that it is possible to be conveyed by words. The union of the opposites in sex is a part of the constitution of nature, which, if any individual member of the human race can dispense with, they are those who should be raised above the Ruler of the universe, and into a greater than God.

"Ah! but," says the objecter, "nobody supposes that there can ever be complete separation of the sexes, but what we do mean is, that the written formula by which their union is consented to will be abolished." Why did you not say that it was the form of marriage that the "Woman Movement" would change, and not marriage itself? In this we agree with you perfectly. It will change, and no further general progress can be attained by the race until it has been changed. It will change, because woman is to be the proud equal of man in all things, and if there is one thing in which a superior should be recognized, it is in this very question of the relation of the sexes, and the superior should be woman.

The ulterior results of the union of the sexes is reproduction of their kind, and we hold that in this matter woman should be the determining power, and whatever there is in present forms of marriage that militates against her supreme right in this respect, we again assert should be changed. The progressive tendencies of the age have denounced the submission of woman to man, and the time, if not already come, will come shortly, in which, with or without the consent and approval of present customs and forms, she will no more submit that a law, no matter how sacredly held, shall bind her to bear children by a man who has taught her to abhor him or whom she holds in disgust.

No such forced associations as present systems compel can ever receive the sanction of God's marriage law. "Whatever God hath joined together let not man put asunder," applies to no such abortions of nature as compel a delicate, sensitive-natured woman to endure the presence of a beastly constitutioned man. Many men are really brutes in nature, and what woman, except she, too, is a beast, can be by God joined to any such? This matter might just as well be considered now as to be forced off; it might be attempted to be put off, but individuality is being developed in women to too great a degree to make such an attempt successful.

While assuming this ultra position we also occupy the other extreme, and declare that of all relations that exist in the universe there are none that should be so holy—so sacred, so reverenced, honored, worshiped—as the true unity—the true marriage—the marriage by God

—of two pure, trusting, loving, equal souls. Before the shrine of such devotion no impurities can kneel; within the influence of such holiness the highest angels come,.and around its temple heaven lingers. Never were any more wide of the mark than when they think we would reduce the relations of the sexes to common looseness. To us there is nothing more revolting in nature than such a condition implies. What we would do, and with all our might, is, to bring the attention of the world—and especially of women—to the realities of marriage, that no relations it presupposes should ever be entered upon, except after the maturest deliberation and the acquisition of the perfect knowledge that God will officiate at the nuptials and approve the union. Of what necessity would laws then be to compel people to live together?

Are we understood? If not, let those who open their mouths to condemn, or those who use their pens to defame, show that they possess the least bit of consistency by withholding the evidence of their ignorance and incapacity. The time is passed for any to manufacture lasting capital by resorting to such methods in the place of reason; and let those who call this a "dirty sheet" examine their specs to see if their surface be not somewhat soiled. "To the pure in heart all things are pure;" to the vile in heart all things are vile, and to the "dirty" in heart all things are dirty. Take this home and consider it, and sleep over it, and wake to the conclusion that we can neither be frightened nor injured by the dirt thrown at us. We shall continue to deal with the conditions of society which we consider behind the times, though the self-constituted conservators of society do array themselves in opposition and denounce us, according to the most approved and respectable style of pharisaical godliness.

The whole tendency, then, of the Woman Question is toward the perfection of the relations between the sexes. It is not to be expected that anything like perfection can be presently attained, but the way to it can be broken, and the conditions of improvement can be instituted; woman can be made free, can be made the mistress of herself, and can be placed in conditions of equality with those who now hold absolute sway over her. We have said before that the Woman Question was not simply a question of suffrage, but a question of humanity, and it is so, because to the perfect relations of the sexes does the future of humanity look for the disposal of the necessity of regeneration. In conclusion we assert that, Whatever God hath joined together no man *can* put asunder—hence the inconsistency of attempting it by the continuation of laws enforcing present marriage customs.

INTOLERANCE AND BIGOTRY; COMMON SENSE AND REASON.

ARBITRARY DISTINCTIONS BELONG TO THE AGE OF BRUTE FORCE.

Notwithstanding the experience the civilized world has had in its pursuit after a better religion and more diffusive science, it still blindly pursues the same courses regarding every fresh question which comes up for solution, with that bigoted opposition that knows and sees nothing but some time-honored custom or revered authority. Those who have arrived at a tolerable liberality in religious matters, through the most bitter opposition, are just as inconsistently bitter to that which is still ahead of them as those who differed from them were to their advanced thought.

It is not a little to be wondered at, that the most inconsistent intolerance and the most determined pharisaical bigotry with which the Woman Question is met, is found inside of the Church. Though, when we remember that there are those still who declare that Joshua commanded the sun to stand still, and that it obeyed, because such an assertion is found within the Bible, it should not appear so terribly strange. So long as there are any who will be led by blind authority, regardless of all use of common sense or reason, so long may the advocates of equality for women expect to meet the most inconsistent opposition from the churches, especially from those which teach that "it is a shame for a woman to speak in church," and that it is the duty of wives to "submit yourselves unto your husbands." The fact that such ideas prevailed centuries ago, is no reason why we should, in these enlightened days, still subscribe to them. The teachings of Jesus himself inculcate the adoption of new ideas. Moses taught, "An eye for an eye," etc., but Jesus taught, "But I say unto you, love your enemies," etc. Thus, on the evidence of their most sacred authority, self-styled Christians are condemned for the unreasonable opposition they show to new truth.

All the means by which science is demonstrated, and all the ways in which new truth is evolved, teach that this recently-begun agitation, called the "Woman Question," is *the* question of the hour. There are others which perhaps some look upon as more important, but if the "Common Sense" and the "Reason" of the age is questioned, they will answer that it is not only the question of the hour, but that it is the gravest of all questions. Upon the relations of the sexes does the future condition of humanity depend. It is these relations which lie at the basis of society, and too long already have they been left to be determined by the blind suggestions of passion; too long has science been denied entry into their realm. In the production of everything that society requires for its subsistence, comfort or pleasure, the lights of science are made constant use of to point the way; but in the much graver matter of the production of society itself, science is denied all entrance, and it is left to be *just what it can*, without government or guide to assist its formation.

There are a certain class of persons who denounce, with holy vehemence, any attempt to show up the conditions of society. The apparent argument is, that to touch anything that is diseased is evidence of the existence of disease in those who perform that operation. Thus, if any argue to show that there are *bad things* in the present structure of society, they are the "dirty" ones, instead of those they touch. The same argument would make those who assail polygamy, polygamists. We often wonder if it were possible for *such* argumentists to be impervious to the feeling of contempt which they call forth from those who understand the situation. They are looked upon just about as one would be to-day who should endeavor to convince the people that the world is a plane instead of a globe. The end of the argument would be that he would convince them, instead, that he was an exceeding simpleton, and more a subject of pity than contempt. So, too, are they who cry "dirt" more worthy of pity than contempt, for they only convince those who are worth seeking to convince that they are a class of very narrow and contracted-in-all-ways minded persons. For all this they assume the most sublime dignity and self-complacent assurance, and tread the world much as though they were saying, "Did not I tell you so?"

The days of arbitrary rule have departed. All things move by the more enlightened rule of equal right. In one department alone does absolute sway still linger. Woman is subjugated still by man; woman, as a sex, is under the absolute sway of man as a sex. All rules of life are by him laid down for her to be guided, governed and condemned by. We flatter ourselves that this America is a free country, in which all enjoy the rights of equality. Not a bit of it. Never were you more thoroughly, more radically mistaken. There is no such thing as female freedom, or female equality, before the law, in the land. Rather, she has less of them, comparatively, than she has in almost any other country. Of this most apparent fact, however, American women are entirely ignorant or purposely oblivious, and sometimes we almost despair of any immediate possibility of an awakening to the reality of the degradation and slavery which a large part of them submit to with such great indifference. However, the fires of liberty are burning upon the altars of many aroused hearts, and these shall be the flames that will spread world-wide, and destroy the vain illusion of a dependent ease which is substituted for independent self-reliance.

THE QUESTION OF DRESS.

NO. I.

THE PHRENOLOGICAL JOURNAL ON WOMEN AT WATERING-PLACES—
IT TELLS ONLY ONE-HALF THE TRUTH—THE MEANING OF DISINCLI-
NATION TO MARRIAGE ON THE PART OF MEN—THE ABSURDITIES OF
PRESENT STYLES OF DRESS—WOMAN'S RIGHT TO DECIDE FOR HER-
SELF.

A writer in the *Phrenological Journal*, in endeavoring to answer the
question, "What makes women unhappy?" says:

At all the watering-places and seaside resorts there has been a no-
ticeable decrease in beaux. Daughters, chaperoned through empty par-
lors, look in vain for that necessary commodity—suitable gentlemen
attendants—while planning mammas grow frantic over the hopeless task
of husband hunting. These mothers and daughters, like many others
elsewhere, are, with all their lack of innate refinement, women of average capacity, who, from lack of occupation, spend the best years of
their lives in trying to entice men, for the sole purpose of having some
one to supply, in a genteel way, the funds required for display.
Night after night these daughters attire themselves in the costumes
remarkable for their scantiness in one direction and abundance in the
other, and expose their persons. unblushingly as they tread the mazes
of the voluptuous dance in the arms of any worn *roue* who may happen to be on hand.
The extravagance of these women keep all honest marriageable
men away from their presence; they are afraid to go even for a few
weeks' pleasure where they are liable to be tempted to marry women

whom they could not possibly support, and so they stay at home wishing all the time they could find some sensible girls who would be content with competency. I wish I could tell these wretched girls how many solid, substantial men are at their places of business this summer, kept at home by their thoughtless conduct, and how very many well-meaning, moderately cultured men are wishing every day for wives, but who see no chance in the present state of society. They don't care to wed a woman whose eyes are familiar with fashionable indecencies, and whose tastes are so perverted that they are willing to let unclean men handle their person in the waltz, or gaze with pleased eyes upon their naked arms and shoulders.

That the above is only one-half the truth, every woman who will be honest enough to say what she knows will testify, while every unmarried man's thoughts are reproduced therein. It was quite "the rage" not many years ago among young men to consider themselves particularly fortunate to be able to carry off these "summer butterflies" as wives. This was when "watering-places" were not so well patronized as they are now, and not for the same purposes. It is getting to be pretty well understood now, that watering-places are stocked with those who are *specially* in the market for sale to the highest bidder ; and that a bid seldom goes unfilled; hence the bidders are few. These facts show a growing indifference on the part of man for marriage, and the showing is anything but promising to such of the female sex as are unprepared to meet the responsibilities and duties of life for themselves.

It is a subject of considerable importance to rightly understand the meaning of these things, and in what it finds its life. There are many reasons assigned, but the root of the matter lies in the growth of freedom in the general heart of man. The mere fact that marriage is considered practically as an indissoluble tie, hinders those who have comprehensive ideas of freedom from entering upon it. It is seen that on all sides there are people bound together by this tie who live lives of utter misery because of it, and that it really becomes the incentive to a deal of demoralization, that would not be so were it not for the shackles it imposes. The day for limitations to be continued upon matters wherein the *individual* is the one primarily interested is nearing its close. The community has no right to impose conditions, or enforce restrictions, upon the individual, which the general good of the community does not demand. The realization of this fact is the real reason of the growing disfavor with which men regard marriage. This is from the male standpoint.

There are other reasons which obtain among a certain portion of women, which assist this disposition on the part of man. Every year there are more and more women becoming individualized—that is, each year a larger proportion of the sex is becoming independent and self-supporting. There are very few women who, once having arrived at the condition of ability to provide for themselves well, will ever sell-themselves to any man for the sake of support. We use the word "sell" in its fullest significance, as meaning an actual transfer for a consideration. A large part of the marriages which are contracted are nothing more nor less than bargains and sales, into which consideration the questions of love and adaptation do not enter. What is more common than to hear women remark, "She has made her market," or, "She has done well?" and what, withal, is more decidedly vulgar?

The truth of the matter is, that "young ladies" are set up, advertised and sold to the highest cash bidder, and where a mutual attraction does not exist, a strict analysis finds no difference between it and the other association of the sexes denominated prostitution. It is true that it is regarded in an entirely different light; but that is equally true of many other things between which there is still less real distinction. Technically speaking, it is a dictinction without a difference, the distinction being that, whereas in the former case it is a transfer—or sale —for life, in the latter it is at the option of the contracting parties, and the lacking of difference being, that both are for a consideration given by the man and received by the woman.

We would not have it understood that we denounce true marriage. We are the most profound believers in those marriages which are made "in heaven," and which man cannot put asunder—that is, in marriages which have the sanction of God and nature, which no marriage of convenience can have. At the same time we confess to being utter disbelievers in marriages which lack this approval. Neither would we have it understood that we sanction prostitution; but, on the contrary, we would assert in the most strenuous, pointed and positive terms, that prostitution, whether practised under the sanction of the law or without it, is a withering, blighting curse upon a woman and a foul blotch upon the fair face of humanity.

We do not quote the above as a text for the discussion of marriage, but for the purpose of considering the matter of dress, which, in connection with woman, has an intimate relation with the question of freedom and equality. A woman rigged with the entire paraphernalia of fashion is only a fit subject for a show. There is so much of artificial ornamentation that nature, whatever her beauties are, retires in disgust, before superfluity on the one extreme and brazenness upon the other. Ladies who would affect to blush when subjects are spoken of which are of the greatest interest to humanity generally, and who would hide their faces behind their handkerchiefs to cover the blushes they would have it supposed were there, appear at balls and receptions and at the opera, with the most perfect self-assurance, virtually naked to the waists, and if by such exposure of their persons some admirer is made bold enough to presume upon it, the " big brother " has business on hand to punish the insult. These things bespeak a superficiality and a mock-modesty that is robbing the sex of all its natural beauty and its real attractiveness.

Practically, the present styles of dress for women of business, so far as convenience is concerned, are simply absurd, not to say ridiculous, while from the health point of view they are suicidal. While women remain mere dolls, to be admired for the external appearance they can present, it does not matter very much how they dress; but when any of them shake off the shackles of dependence, and become their own support, they should certainly have the right to accommodate their dress to their new modes of life, without being exposed to the ridicule of the fashion apes of either sex. In this view of the question we challenge any one to offer a single reasonable argument in favor of the skirts now universally worn by women, but, on the contrary, we assert that they are open to objection from every point of consideration.

There are no limitations, either of law or custom, against men dressing to suit the business they are engaged in. Neither should there be against the same right for women. Therefore we protest against all laws and all customs which place limitations upon the rights of women to change their present styles of dressing so as to meet the reasonable demands of their growing freedom and independence. In our next we shall consider some of the special objections to present fashions.

THE QUESTION OF DRESS.

NO. II.

THE SIXTEENTH AMENDMENT; ITS RELATION TO AND EFFECT UPON
"DRESS"—PRESENT STYLES RUINOUS TO HEALTH—THE NECESSITY
OF MODIFICATIONS TO MEET THE DEMANDS OF WOMAN'S NEW
SPHERES OF ACTION.

It may be thought far-fetched, by some, to assert that the subject
of dress has any legitimate bearing upon the Sixteenth Amendment
Question; if so, it comes from lack of thought and attention to the
many-sided bearings of the Woman Question. Taken as a whole, it
must be considered as one of the most important Humanitarian movements of the age, and every part of it which is not already based on
fixed principles of right, or upon demonstrated facts, should be analyzed,
to the end that *the right* may be separated from *the wrong*, so that the
latter may be discarded or supplanted by something better. It is more
than a privilege ; it is more than a right—it is a duty, stern and imper-
ative, that if there are any hindrances hanging around, which prevent
the legitimate use of their newly-acquired freedom, woman should shake
them off.

But how does dress relate to woman's freedom? We have said
that it was impossible for a single argument to be offered in favor of the
style of skirts now almost universally worn by women of refinement
and intelligence (?) and just as little for all other external parts of their
dress. One of the first principles of dress, regarding health, is, *that all
portions of the body should ⌐e evenly coverd*, so that there shall always
be a free and uninf⌐ nced circulation of blood. As women dress
now, the great am⌐ ₋nt of clothing worn about the lumbar regions of
the body, which at all times keeps that portion of the body warm, even

when the extremities may be nearly frozen, produces a powerful determination of blood to those parts. These parts being a large part of the time kept at a very much higher temperature than any other portion of the body, the extremities are deprived of the vitality requisite to continue healthy conditions. It is a well known fact, that since the present fashions of padding and bustle-wearing came in vogue, the class of complaints known as Female Weakness have increased a hundred fold. While it would not be true that this increase is entirely owing to this overheating process, it is true that it will reasonably account for a very large proportion of it. And when we remember that with this overdress of central parts of the body, the neck, shoulders, and upper parts of the breast and back have been almost deprived of covering, which, when allowed, has been of the nearest approach to nothing, we need not wonder that there are so many frail women, weakly wives, and fragile or scrubby children.

The same is also true of the dressing of the feet, which, of all parts of the body, can least bear uneven exposure. A person may possess vitality enough to bear the exposure of the upper parts of the body, which are near the centre of circulation; but a person who has cold feet habitually, cannot retain health for any length of time, and with women nothing is more conducive to all forms of irregularities than this foolish, criminal practice of light dressing for the feet and ankles.

These practices, if allowable or reasonable at all for women of fashion, who are never obliged to expose themselves, cannot be tolerated a moment by the sensible business woman. She requires the same degree of protection, and even more care, than man; but women who, from choice or necessity, become regularly attendant upon business, have not, as a rule, been sensible enough, or independent enough, to meet the situation. What is more common of a rainy morning or evening than to see hundreds of shop women going to, or returning from, business, with nothing but thin-soled, lasting gaiters on their feet, and with wet skirts draggling their limbs? If this is morning, they remain all day in this condition, which practice, continued sufficiently long, will in every case produce its legitimate results.

Again: What sense is there in long skirts for business women at any time. 'Tis true that they are pretty nearly all the dressing or protection the lower limbs have; but what kind of protection? Sufficient, perhaps, when worn for nothing but to hide the limbs, but what against dampness, dust and the bleak wintry winds. Against these, clothing more nearly adjusted to the limbs is required; so that it comes down to this at last: that long skirts are worn, not for clothing, but for the purpose of hiding the limbs. Dress is either for the purpose of protection or for disguise. If for the last—and it is indelicate or revolting to the nature of woman to so dress her legs that they can be free to perform the functions of locomotion—why should it not be just as indelicate to go with arms naked to the shoulder, as thousands do who would scream if their leg to the knee were exposed? And why should it not be considered a hundred fold more indelicate to expose, virtually, their breasts to the waist, as thousands do, than it is to tastefully and reasonably dress their legs?

The fact of the case in this matter of female dress is, that a blind and foolish custom has decreed that women must wear skirts to hide their legs, while they may, almost *ad libitum*, expose their arms and breasts. For our part, we can see no more indelicacy in a properly clad leg than in a properly clad arm; but we can see a deal of sentimental and hypocritical mock modesty in the custom which demands skirts and allows bare arms, shoulders and breasts. It is time to call things by their right names, and to be honest enough to speak the truth about these things, which are fettering and diseasing women and producing a generation of sickly children. If those who affect a great deal more modesty and delicacy than they are willing to allow that those have who are bold enough to discuss this question truthfully, vent their spleen and show their virtuous indignation, by calling us bad names, we simply assure them that our estimation of truth, and our desire to promote the true interests of our sex, rises far above all care for whatever they may say or think, and that we are perfectly willing to intrust the vindication of our course to the next ten years, when such unsightly and health-destroying things as our present system of dressing presents will be among the things which were.

What we have said thus far upon this subject may be considered as simply suggestive, when compared with what might be said in direct attack upon the system from the standpoint of delicacy. We have often been in stores when it became necessary for the female employee to climb a step-ladder to obtain articles of goods from high shelvings; and we have often witnessed the exposure of ladies getting into omnibusses; in either of which cases, had they been properly and judiciously dressed, they would have been the extreme of delicacy compared with what they were; and hence it is that we reassert, that the system prescribed by present custom has nothing to recommend it, but everything to denounce it. When women take the equality which we are showing they are entitled to under our Constitution, just as it now is, it is to be hoped that they will also exercise the right to dress themselves according to the requirements of their callings, even if that demands the proscription of skirts with which women have been dragged to death so many years.

The *World* says: "The average weight, all the year round, of that portion of woman's clothing which is supported from the waist, is between ten and fifteen pounds. Are weak backs a wonder? Put on suspenders, girls!"

CONSTITUTIONAL EQUALITY.

STARTLING ANNUNCIATION — A NEW POLITICAL PLATFORM PRO-
CLAIMED—WOMAN'S RIGHT OF SUFFRAGE FULLY RECOGNIZED IN
THE CONSTITUTION AND COMPLETELY ESTABLISHED BY POSITIVE
LAW AND RECENT EVENTS—THE SIXTEENTH AMENDMENT A DEAD
LETTER—CANDIDATE FOR THE PRESIDENCY IN 1872.

[The progressive world has been considerably aroused and set to
thinking by the second pronunciamento of Victoria C. Woodhull,
which, as it has a direct connection with these articles, is here presented
in full :]

In my address to the people, published on the 2d of April last, an-
nouncing myself a candidate for the Presidency of the United States
in 1872, I called their attention to the disorganized condition of parties,
and briefly commented upon the issues which were most likely to require a settlement by that election.

I pointed to the changed sentiment which had brought the negro
from slavery to freedom, and raised him to equal political rights.

I alluded to the aspirations of woman for complete recognition of
equality of right, socially and politically, as *intended in her creation and
announced by Divine Word that she should enjoy.*

I stated that these aspirations had caused the question to exist,
whether this equality should be longer denied, and that its issue would
be tried and settled before the next Presidential election.

I knew then that woman's complete political equality with man
had been provided for and secured by our fathers in the Federal Constitution; that its entire exercise could not, be denied under it one mo-

ment after it should be permitted in any State of the Union, and that when permitted in one it would be legal in all. The time had not come for this announcement. It was necessary that woman should agitate the question of her rights, that its clear bearing and all that it covered of social or political advantage should be fully comprehended and appreciated. This agitation has been made in the claim for "The Sixteenth Amendment."

Under the discussion of this claim, the knowledge and appreciation of her rights has developed. In the period required for this discussion, the irrefragable evidence of their complete legal recognition has come forth.

As I have been the first to comprehend these Constitutional and legal facts, so am I the first to proclaim, as *I now do proclaim, to the women of the United States of America, that they are enfranchised.* That they are, by the Constitution of the Union, by the recognition of its Congress, by the action of a State, by the exercise of its functions, henceforth entitled in all the States of the Union, and in all its territories, *to free and equal suffrage with men.*

This has been established by Wyoming. In the elections therein held women voted. By their votes an election was made perfect, they having thus, in the language of Sec. 2, Art. I., of the Constitution, the "QUALIFICATIONS REQUISITE FOR ELECTORS OF THE MOST NUMEROUS BRANCH OF THE STATE LEGISLATURE"—which branch, as well as the State Senate and members of Congress, were elected by their co-operative suffrage with men. Thus one of the requisite conditions of the Federal Constitution was fulfilled, and *it is the most important of all,* for it is the culminating or closing one by which all are made perfect in the joining and blending together in one act the *independent,* though legally *precedent, State act,* with the Federal condition and act, to secure an inalienable right of suffrage to the women of Wyoming. Their members of Congress are their direct representatives in that body. Their Senators are again their representatives as consolidated through a legislative vote for a longer period—the legislative vote directly dependent upon the vote of the people for the legislative *existence* of the voters.

This brings us to a further condition of the Constitution, namely, the last clause of Article V., which is, "THAT NO STATE, WITHOUT ITS CONSENT, SHALL BE DEPRIVED OF ITS EQUAL SUFFRAGE IN THE SENATE." It follows that if one State by the votes of women elect a Legislature which, by its constitutional functions, elects senators of the United States, and that other States do not, that the absolute elementary principle of equal suffrage therein is lost, unless each State not so represented shall, by an *act of its whole people*, *"consent"* thereto.

From this exercise of female suffrage in Wyoming comes the legal, the undeniable fact, that each State has now imposed upon it the necessity, *not of granting* the right of suffrage to woman, for it exists, but of denying it if it is to be restrained—but how ! Not by a legislative act, that is not sufficient, but by a convention, with its act to be approved by a vote of the *people* of whom the women would be voters also ! Until a denial is accomplished in this manner woman HAS now, and will retain, *the right of suffrage in every State and Territory of this Union.*

A woman is as much a *"citizen"* in all that relates to *"life, liberty and independence"*—in all that relates to property and personal protection, under the Federal and State Constitutions, under the National and State laws—as man is or can be.

This being so, *and it cannot be gainsaid,* the question is forever settled by Article IV. of the Federal Constitution, Sec. 2, first clause, which says : THE CITIZENS OF EACH STATE SHALL BE ENTITLED TO ALL THE PRIVILEGES AND IMMUNITIES OF CITIZENS IN THE SEVERAL STATES."

That the framers of the Constitution had Woman's Rights clearly in their minds is borne out by its whole structure. Nowhere is the word *man* used in contradistinction to *woman*. They avoided both terms and used the word "persons" for the same reason as they avoided the word "slavery," namely, to prevent an untimely contest over rights which might prematurely be discussed to the injury of the infant republic.

Our political fathers believed in the Word of God—they knew that he had said, "I have created man and woman in my own image," that "God blessed them and said unto them, be fruitful and multiply and replenish the earth and subdue it and have dominion over it." Jointly was this done, with equal right; no superiority to the male, but a perfect equality in all things was recognized ; and what "God thus joined" they dared not attempt to sunder, and did not, but recognized the Divine Word as their guide in forming a perfect equality for "male and female " under the Constitution made through them by Divine guidance for the rule, government and blessings of future generations.

The issue upon the question of female suffrage being thus definitely settled, and its rights inalienably secured to woman, a brighter future

7

dawns upon the country. Woman can now unite in purifying the elements of political strife—in restoring the government to pristine integrity, strength and vigor. To do this, many reforms become of absolute necessity. Prominent in these are:

A complete reform in the Congressional and Legislative work, by which all political discussion shall be banished from legislative halls, and debate be limited to the actual business of the people.

A complete reform in Executive and Departmental conduct, by which the President and the Secretaries of the United States, and the Governors and State officers, shall be forced to recognize that they are the servants of the people, appointed to attend to the business of the people, and not for the purpose of perpetuating their official positions, or of securing the plunder of public trusts for the enrichment of their political adherents and supporters.

A reform in the tenure of office, by which the Presidency shall be limited to one term, with a retiring life pension, and a permanent seat in the Federal Senate, where his Presidential experience may become serviceable to the nation, and on the dignity and life emolument of Presidential Senator he shall be placed above all other political positions, and be excluded from all professional pursuits.

A reform in our financial relations, by which the public debt shall become the security, and the basis representation of a national currency—the one exchangeable for the other, as required for use or interest investment—and · when currency is taken out for a deposit of national debt, all interest to cease on the sum of the latter so deposited, until it is again issued for currency paid in lieu thereof.

A reform in the method of intercommunication between the States, by which railroad corporations shall not extend their ownership to lines of railway beyond the State which gave them existence, and by which the general government, in use of its postal powers, shall secure the transportation of through mails, passengers and merchandise upon physically connecting or locally relating lines of roads at fair rates of compensation; and due safeguard for life and property be enforced; and also to destroy one of the fertile sources of corrupt influences in State Legislature, by imposing the condition that all members of the National and State Legislative bodies shall, by law, have the right of free passage over any railroad in their respective States.

A complete reform in commercial and navigation laws, by which American ships and American seamen shall be practically protected by the admission of all that is required for construction of the first, or the use and maintenance of either, free in bond or on board, and that only American registered ships, entitled thereto by home building, by capture, or purchased after stranding and American repairs, shall have the privilege and protection of the American flag.

. A reform between the relations of the employer and employed, by which shall be secured the practice of the great natural law, of one-third of time to labor, one-third to recreation and one-third to rest, that by this intellectual improvement and physical development may go on to that perfection which the Almighty Creator designed.

A reform in the principles of protection and revenue, by which the largest home and foreign demand shall be created and sustained for products of American industry of every kind—by which this industry shall be freed from the ruinous competition of the class-created, class-oppressed pauper labor of Europe—by which shall be secured that constant employment to American workingmen and working women which never fails—by developing skill to reduce average costs in products to a minimum value—to bring competency to the employed, and unlimited national wealth upon which the ratio of taxation for government expense becomes insignificant in amount, and no burden to the people.

A reform in the system of crime punishment, by which the death penalty shall no longer be inflicted—by which the hardened criminal shall have no human chance of being let loose to harass society until the term of the sentence, whatever that may be, shall have expired, and by which, during that term, the entire prison employment shall be for—and the product thereof be faithfully paid over to—the support of the criminal's family, instead of being absorbed by the legal thieves to whom, in most cases, the administration of prison discipline has been intrusted, and by whom atrocities are perpetrated in the secrecy of the prison inclosure, which, were they revealed, would shock the moral sense of all mankind.

In the broadest sense, I claim to be the friend of equal rights, a faithful worker in the cause of human advancement; and more espec-. ially the friend, supporter, co-laborer with those who strive to encourage the poor and the friendless—who patiently and zealously, day and night, toil to promote the cause of labor, to secure to the great masses of working people, "male and female," their rights and their rewards. I claim from these, and from all others in the social scale, that support in the bold political course I have taken, which shall give me the strength and the position to carry out the needed reforms, which shall secure to them in return, the blessings which the Creator designed the human race should enjoy.

If I obtain this support, and by it the position of President of the United States, I promise that woman's strength and woman's will, with God's support, if he vouchsafe it, shall open to them, and to this country, a new career of greatness in the race of nations, which can only be secured by that fearless course of truth from which the nations of the earth, under despotic male governments, have so far departed.

V. C. W.

NEW YORK, Nov. 19, 1870.

In accordance with the above, we shall assume the new position that the of rights women under the Constitution are complete, and hereafter we shall contend, not for a Sixteenth Amendment to the Constitution, but that the Constitution already recognizes women as citizens, and that they are justly entitled to all the privileges and immunities of citizens.

It will therefore be our duty to call on women everywhere to come boldly forward and exercise the right they are thus guaranteed. It is not to be expected that men who assume that they alone, as citizens of the United States, are entitled to all the immunities and privileges guaranteed by the Constitution, will consent that women may exercise the right of suffrage until they are compelled ; and without doubt the highest judicial tribunal of the country will be obliged to give its decision in woman's favor before men will allow women this privilege. Already quite a number of "*gallants*" have exhibited altogether too much fiendish delight to make us hopeful that they will yield grace fully. They retort, when we pin them down to the letter of the Constitution, by saying in substance : "Get us to acknowledge your Constitutional right if you can, and that you will have to do before you can vote." Such is the opposition we shall have to confront and conquer; for, believing as we do that we are now being debarred from privileges which rightfully belong to us, we will never cease the struggle until they are recognized, and we see women established in their true position of equality with the *rest of the citizens* of the United States.

CONSTITUTIONAL EQUALITY.

NO. II.

WOMEN ARE CITIZENS OF THE UNITED STATES AND OF THE STATE
IN WHICH THEY RESIDE—KEEP IT BEFORE THE PEOPLE.

1. "THAT ALL PERSONS BORN OR NATURALIZED IN THE UNITED
STATES, AND SUBJECT TO THE JURISDICTION THEREOF, ARE CITIZENS
OF THE UNITED STATES AND OF THE STATE IN WHICH THEY RE-
SIDE."

2. "THAT CITIZENS OF EACH STATE SHALL BE ENTITLED TO
ALL THE PRIVILEGES AND IMMUNITIES OF CITIZENS IN THE SEVERAL
STATES."

3. "THAT NO STATE WITHOUT ITS CONSENT SHALL BE DE-
PRIVED OF ITS EQUAL SUFFRAGE IN THE SENATE." And

4. That as the women citizens of Wyoming do possess the "QUALI-
FICATIONS REQUISITE FOR ELECTORS OF THE MOST NUMEROUS BRANCH
OF THE STATE LEGISLATURE," through which they obtain suffrage in
the Senate, it follows that the citizens of each State, though entitled to
the privileges and immunities of citizens in the several States, are debarred from exercising these privileges and enjoying these immunities,
and, therefore, that the United States does not guarantee to every State
a common form of Republican Government.

Such are a few of the declarations of the Organic Law of the country, which point out the inconsistencies which mark the administration
of so-called government, but which would be much better defined were
it called tyranny instead.

One very learned "limb' of the law" declared that there was nothing in the Constitution 'that could be construed into recognizing women as citizens in the full sense of that word as applied to men. We called his attention to Section 1, Article XIV., of Amendments to the Constitution, and desired him to interpret the following language : " ALL PERSONS BORN OR NATURALIZED IN THE UNITED STATES AND SUBJECT TO THE JURISDICTION THEREOF, ARE CITIZENS OF THE UNITED STATES AND OF THE STATE WHEREIN THEY RESIDE."

" Oh," replied he, " that's unconstitutional, and will be so declared by the Supreme Court of the United States before ten years; and," continued he, " suppose that is in the Constitution, every State has the right to determine for itself who shall vote ;" and cited several States where constitutions say every " male citizen," etc. We then requested him to complete reading the section, which is as follows: " NO STATE SHALL MAKE OR ENFORCE ANY LAW WHICH SHALL ABRIDGE THE PRIVILEGES OR IMMUNITIES OF CITIZENS OF THE UNITED STATES."

Now, if women are persons, are they not also citizens ? and if citizens, no *State has any* RIGHT to enforce *any* LAW that shall deprive them of THE RIGHT OF SUFFRAGE, which is one of the privileges of all citizens.

" But," says another, " Congress did not intend by the said amendment 'to include women ;' but they did define, fully and unmistakably who are citizens." Now, if it can be proved that women are not "persons," it can then be said that women are not entitled to all the privileges of citizens of the United States, and consequently that they are not entitled to suffrage. Unless this can be done, we shall hold that the *women of the United States are already enfranchised.*

States may and should prescribe the duties of citizens to make themselves recognizable by the administrators of the law, but they have no right to completely abridge the right of any citizen of legal age to vote.

This aspect of the case entirely changes the programme which women should pursue to obtain the exercise of the right of suffrage. Every woman who desires to exercise this right, which we have shown is hers, *should comply with all the prescribed preliminaries for voting, and should, at the next election for officers in the State in which they severally reside, use their utmost endeavors to cast their votes,* which being debarred from doing, they should, every one of them, appeal to the necessary legal or judicial tribunals, for the required redress of the denial of rights the Constitution grants them as individuals. It is time now for every woman who feels the condition of servitude in which the sex has been restrained so long, to arouse to the necessities of the situation, and to never cease the struggle until their full guaranteed constitutional rights are accorded to them by man, and they are fully secured in the exercise of them.

There seems to be a peculiar sensitiveness on the part of a large majority of men regarding this matter of suffrage for women. They exhibit the same spirit that the slaveholders of the South used to exhibit when the right of slavery was questioned. Let the question be broached, and straightway they fire up, and show evident symptoms of a design to demolish somebody. The question touches them in a very tender place, and they wince whenever they are touched. Will you explain, gentlemen, why it is that you exhibit so much uneasiness about this matter? The slaveholder had something that emancipation was to take from him. What is it that you have that emancipation of women is going to take from you? Think of it as you may; try to evade it if you can; attempt to ignore it if you will, men do regard women as their subjects, not to say their slaves, and, therefore, when we talk of freedom it touches a power they have exercised over us, which is one they will no sooner give up than the South would give up their negroes. The questions are parallel.

The Fifteenth Amendment has additional saving power. It is as follows:

" The right of citizens of the United States to vote shall not be denied or abridged by the United States, or by any State, on account of race, color or PREVIOUS CONDITION OF SERVITUDE."

We should be glad to have some of the exalted political authorities of the country inform us wherein the condition of servitude the negro was the subject of differed from the servitude of which woman is the subject, except in the degree in which it was maintained? What constituted slavery for the negro? He was obliged to render involuntary service to a master, for which he generally received no compensation other than the common necessities to support life. He had no right guaranteed him to acquire, hold or convey property. He was subject to the arbitrary will of his master, who became such to him by birth or purchase, and he was not a recognized citizen.

Theoretically, most of the conditions which constituted the negro the slave do not apply to unmarried women; so long as they remain single they are in a partial sense free, and do have the rights to compensation for service rendered, to acquire, hold and convey property, and are not subject to the arbitrary control of any. The moment the woman becomes the wife the conditions are changed wonderfully. The wife is not entitled to compensation for service rendered except to the extent of the common necessities of her station in life. The condition of many negroes in this respect was to be preferred to that of many wives, who are compelled to labor day, week, month and year, to have their compensation taken possession of and controlled by their husbands, who have the right to use it or spend it in whatever way they may decide; for this there is no redress except to separate from their masters, and by so doing be enabled to obtain partial control of themselves ; though this must be without the protection of law.

In some States the wife is held to be property by the law ; if we mistake not, the old English law which makes the wife the subject of attachment and sale is still in force in this State. It is in but a very few of the States that a married woman has the right to acquire, hold and convey property in her own right, and in these few it has been lately granted ; and in all she is subject to the arbitrary will of her master, who is named husband, who can, if he desire, compel her to endure all manner of indignity, and to conform to all his numerous requirements, whether such conformity is her choice or her necessity.

Though a declared citizen of the United States and of the State in which she resides, woman is in various ways denied the freedom, privileges and immunities which are guaranteed to other citizens. The class of privileges and immunities, and the kind of freedom specially referred to here, may be well illustrated by the practice of public hotels, which are bound to extend their hospitality to all citizens who comply with the requirements of law and order. Any man can apply at any hotel in the United States, at any hour of the day or night, and without question he is admitted to the hospitalities of it. But let a strange woman apply at our so-called first-class hotels, and unless she carries a certificate of character with her, which will be closely inspected, or she is introduced by a respectable (?) gentleman acquaintance—personal or by common report—of the hotel, she is liable to the indignities of being denied admission. Thus, while every man, though known to be what is considered disreputable in woman, is admitted to, and protected in, the hospitality for which hotels receive the protection of the law, woman, unless traveling with endorsements, is obliged to submit to the indignity of being classed among the abandoned. Many cases of this kind have come to our knowledge lately, and we shall, when opportunity permits, give the circumstances in detail, with the names both of the women thus treated and of the hotels so treating them.

It is well known that this is the practice of nearly all hotels, and we are determined to know whether the same law that protects hotel-keepers in their pursuit will not compel them to extend their accommodations to all applicants, female as well as male, and protect them so long as they comply with the common rules of hotels, and conduct themselves with decency and propriety. We are determined to know whether they have the right to discriminate as to the character of their guests, and whether the female citizens of the United States and of the States in which they reside, are to be considered guilty until so proven. Even the person under arrest, charged with a heinous crime, is considered innocent until proven guilty by a jury of his peers, by whom he is entitled to be tried and convicted before any one has the right to declare him guilty of the crime charged against him.

There are many other conditions in which women are made exceptions to the common laws of the land, the discrimination always being against her and favorable to man; these extend all the way up from the smallest uses and customs of the times to the denial of right to a voice in the laws of the land to which she, equally with man, is amenable. All of them are so many conditions of servitude, when considered in the strictly analytic sense and according to the letter of the law; they are conditions of inferiority—of compelled servility—and hence it is that on account of woman having been the subject of these conditions, the United States nor any State has the right to deny or abridge her right to vote.

Congress should have made a restricting clause in the Fifteenth Amendment if it were not the intention to include women. Why did they not make it to read, The right of male citizens, etc., etc.? If this were only intended to cover the negro, what is the position of the female of the colored race under it? Hers was, according to common interpretation, a "condition of servitude," and she was of the previously proscribed race and in color black. Besides, she is a person who was born in the United States and subject to the jurisdiction thereof, and consequently is a citizen of the United States and of the State in which she resides.

Thus being a citizen of the United States, neither the United States nor any State shall deny or abridge her right to vote. This denial of right should have been made expressly against women if Congress did not intend to enfranchise the females who had been slaves.

Thus every step taken in analyzing the Constitution of the United States makes it clearer and better defined that women are not only citizens of the United States and of the State in which they reside, but that they are enfranchised and equal with men; or, in other words, that our mothers, sisters and daughters stand on a footing of perfect equality before the political law of the land with our fathers, brothers and sons.

CONSTITUTIONAL EQUALITY.

NO. III.

[We present the following, which is the best of many similar arguments we are in receipt of against our position regarding the Constitutional guarantees to women citizens:]

NEW YORK, November 21, 1870.

MESDAMES WOODHULL & CLAFLIN:

Permit me to say that you misconstrue that part of the Constitution of the United States which reads—"That no State, without its consent, shall be deprived of its equal suffrage in the Senate." What is here meant is the vote of two, which each State, through its senators, has in the Senate. The word State is not used in the Constitution for the citizens as individuals, but for the people as an aggregate or corporate body, except when it is used to denote the territory or both people and territory.

"All persons born or naturalized in the United States and subject to the jurisdiction thereof, are citizens of the United States and citizens of the State wherein they reside.' But this does not make them voters; if it did, the smallest child would have the right of suffrage. Children are citizens and not necessarily voters. Women are citizens and not necessarily voters.

"The citizens of each State shall be entitled to all privileges and immunities of citizens in the several States." "No State shall make or enforce any law which shall abridge the privileges or immunities of citizens of the United States."

The right of suffrage is not a privilege common to all citizens in any State. In no one is a child a voter.

The words privilege and right are not synonymous. A privilege is a law made in favor of an individual or set of individuals. If a privilege becomes common to all, it thereby ceases to be a privilege. A right may belong to all or only to a part.

The women of Wyoming have no suffrage in the Senate of the United States. As already stated, it is the State or States which have suffrage there through the voices of their senators; each State, no matter how big or how little, having two voices and no more than two.

In order that a State may have a republican form of government, it is not necessary that all its citizens should have the right of suffrage.

I call your attention to the above that you may examine into the exact meaning of the Constitution. When you have done this, it is probable that you will conclude that to obtain the right of suffrage you must secure the adoption of the Sixteenth Amendment, or its equivalent, from the several States. Respectfully, etc.,

JAMES M. McKINLEY.

And such is the negative sum total of the constitutional argument against the rights of women citizens of the United States and of the several States comprising it. Let it be distinctly borne in mind that it is *purely negative* from beginning to end, while the enumeration of the privileges and immunities of citizens, the requisite qualifications of electors, and the definition of who are citizens in the Constitution *are all positive.* In general reply, we would ask our correspondent why this discrimination under the Constitution is made as against women; why should it not have been made against man instead; and why should not the women citizens of the United States, they being in the majority, now declare that they, instead of man, are the enfranchised class? We would also respectfully ask, What kind of a republican form of government is that which the minority of a country's citizens formulate?

We perfectly agree with our correspondent that "the word State is not used in the Constitution for the citizens as individuals, but for the people as an aggregate body" of individuals, of which, if we are not entirely without our senses, women form just as important a part as the self-constituted rulers do. A State does not mean the territory comprised within certain geographical limits, but the citizens who occupy these limits; and as women, alike with men, are citizens, and with men occupy these limits, so too are they represented in the Senate, where they are not denied the right of voting. It therefore follows that in a State where both the male and female citizens do vote, the aggregate of individuals obtain representation in the Senate; but in a State where its female citizens are denied the right of voting, the aggregate of citizens comprising the State do not obtain representation in the Senate of the United States—only a part of such aggregate, who do not make up the whole State, are represented, and hence such a State does not possess a republican form of government. Our correspondent says: "The women of Wyoming have no suffrage in the Senate of the United States." We would ask him whether the women of Wyoming would have suffrage in the Senate provided they, voting an entirely separate ticket from the men, should elect a majority of the State Senate and Legislature, and they in their capacity should elect a woman as senator, and she should sit in the Senate Chamber and vote with other senators? Such a contingency would be possible under the present equal enjoyment of rights. and privileges in the State of Wyoming; and when viewed regardless of the influences of precedents of custom, fully and forever establishes the fact that all the citizens of all States are entitled to equal exercise of rights with the citizens of Wyoming, under that provision of the Constitution which provides " That no State shall, without its consent, be deprived of its equal suffrage in the Senate."

" Children are citizens and not necessarily voters. Women are citizens and not necessarily voters." Is all this quite true? Are women, as citizens, denied the right of voting for the same reasons that children are? Children, until they arrive at what is made lawful age, do not possess the common rights of adults outside of voting. At certain ages they are not held responsible as citizens for the result of their action—their parents stand responsible. They cannot hold nor convey property in their own right—their guardians must do it for them. The common privileges and rights of citizens are denied to children, BOTH MALE AND FEMALE, until it is presumed that they have arrived at years of discretion, until which they are subject to the will of their parents, and can be made to obey that will. Is this the argument our correspondent would advance to show that women should not exercise the right of voting? Would he class women as always minors, and say in practice that they never arrive at years of discretion? Would he have it that the Constitution thus stigmatizes women? The States do provide a lawful age, which all adult citizens, male and female, are agreed upon; but when that age shall have been attained by females, there is no power but the usurped and arbitrarily exercised power of man, which denies them the right of exercising what should be a common right for all citizens who have arrived at lawful age, having attained which they are admitted to the common privileges of citizens, such as the right to hold office, to serve as jurors, &c., &c., from which children are debarred. We do not say that children too are not deprived of their rights under the Constitution, but we are just now arguing that women are; at another time the rights of children will be considered

There can be no foundation found in the Constitution for denying the common rights of citizens to any citizen of any State, except upon forfeiture by individual action; and such denial, therefore, is as purely a usurpation of power over women by men as that would be were a single person able to subject the United States to his control, which would be just as much a republican form of government in principle as that is which denies women the common rights of other citizens.

We do not agree with our correspondent's definition of privilege and right. A "right" is something inherent within the individual. A privilege is something that can be extended to the individual; and a government which denies the first or abridges the last is not a government founded in the equality but in the inequality of its citizens. We hold that our government is based on the equality of all its citizens, and, therefore, that the provisions for its administration should be regulated by the equal expression of all the rights of equality by all. A privilege is something that is granted to individuals for specific reasons which should have two considerations: primarily, of benefit to the individual seeking it, and secondarily, to the public by the exercise thereof. Now, voting, or rather the process by which the making and administering of law for the good of the public is obtained, is either a right or a privilege. If it is the former, it is something that can neither be given nor taken away, but is simply suppressed where a portion of the citizens are prevented by the other portion from its exercise. If it is the latter, and it is denied by a portion of the citizens to another portion of them, it is an exercise on their part of arbitrary power which, if it is not actually denied by the Constitution, cannot be justified by any construction or any part thereof. Kings are not the only rulers who can and do exercise arbitrary power which is not derived from the people. Women are forced to contribute to the support of government in every way that men are, but at the same time are prevented from having any voice whatever in it. If this is not the exercise of arbitrary power without any consent whatever on their part, we should be made happy by having our fallacy pointed out. If it is the exercise of power without their consent, we should also be made happy to have some shrewd political authority point out wherein our government is republican in form as administered on the part of thirty-six of the thirty-seven States which constitute its various organic members.

If it is not necessary that all the citizens of a State should have the right of suffrage in order that it may have a republican form of government, what part of such citizens is it necessary should have such right in order to give it that form. If one-half of a State's citizens do possess the right of suffrage, and the State thereby becomes republican in form, why may not one-fourth of the citizens formulate a republican form of government? if one-fourth can, why cannot one-tenth or one-hundredth or one-thousandth part do the same? If this is a matter of arbitrary distinction, why not have the distinction distinctly asserted, so that a few of the citizens of no State could seize upon its government and say that it was still republican in form, and that in permitting it to continue Congress was guaranteeing to the people of such a State a republican form of government? Or is a republican form of government a form that is sufficiently strong to maintain itself against all civil opposition, and that because the part of the citizens of the United States who are debarred from exercising their right to govern themselves are too weak to assert their rights that the government is republican in form? Which horn of the dilemma will our self-constituted rulers take?

We are not attempting to interpret the meaning of the Constitution of the United States; we are taking it just as it stands and according to what it says. We can understand what it says, but if it mean something that it does not say, we must at once confess not only our inability to interpret it but also our disinclination. If so important an instrument as the Constitution of our country must need be interpreted to find out its meaning, we think it high time that it should be remodeled and made so plain there could be no mistaking its provisions; besides, there is danger that the time may come when a sufficient number may interpret it differently from those of you who are now debarring women from exercising the rights of citizens to self-government, to rise to the point of asserting their rights somewhat differently from what they are doing now.

If the Government of the United States intend to prevent one-half its citizens from having any voice in its councils, let it at once come to the point and amend the Constitution, by providing that women shall not be entitled to vote, and thus prevent the women citizens of Wyoming from exercising rights which the women citizens of every other State are prevented from doing.

The Constitution, in declaring who are citizens, and in providing for a government to emanate from them, was evidently better legislation than was known or thought. But such has been the result. The silent acquiescence of women to the arbitrary authority of men was so complete that the framers of the Constitution so penned its provisions that women are now enabled to come forward and claim their rights under it, they having grown into an appreciation of them. Rights which are not appreciated may as well not exist, but rights appreciated should never be withheld by any government from any of its citizens. Sec. 2 of Art. XI. provides "That each State shall appoint, in such manner as the Legislature thereof may direct, a number of electors equal to the whole number of senators and representatives to which the State may be entitled in Congress." By the State it is evidently meant its citizens, and the number of its representatives is determined by the number of such citizens. When we pass to Sec. 2 of Art. XIV., of Amendments to the Constitution, we find this construction still further favored, for therein it provides that "Indians not taxed," and "male persons to whom is denied the right to vote," shall not form a part of such basis of representation. These provisions, taken in connection with Art. I. of Sec 4 of Art. I. of the Constitution, which provides that "The *times, places* and *manner* of holding elections for senators and representatives shall be prescribed in each State, but the Congress may, at any time, by law, make or alter such regulations, except as to the places of choosing senators," evidently vests the determining power regarding elections in Congress, and the legitimate inference is that the basis of representation is also the basis from which government shall emanate, this basis being all citizens of the United States. The times, places and manner of holding election, is given to States subject to Congress, but this does not say that the States may debar citizens of the United States from co-operating in such elections.

When any special provisions are made, the discrimination is distinctly marked, as between males and females, which legitimately leaves the construction of all the rest of the Constitution to be made to apply to citizens without regard to sex.

We have thus specifically considered the objections made by our correspondent to our position regarding the necessity of a sixteenth amendment to the Constitution. We do not infer from his communication that he is opposed to female equality, but that he considers it necessary to amend the Constitution before women can exercise the right to vote. Before the women citizens of Wyoming obtained the recognition of their right to vote, the common construction of the Constitution, strengthened by long practice and custom, might have made it requisite to obtain an amendment, but, as the rights of citizens of the United States in each of the States should be equal, that necessity did not exist after this recognition in Wyoming.

Finally, we call attention to the construction of the Fifteenth Amendment. " *The right of citizens of the United States to vote* shall not be denied or abridged by the United States or by any State on account of race, color or previous condition of servitude." From this it would seem that the rights of citizens of the United States to vote had been denied and abridged, on account of race, color or previous condition of servitude by the United States; or that there were citizens of the United States who, having the right to vote, from cause did not exercise that right, which was the exact condition of the negro. There can be but one inference from the language of this Amendment, and that inference is, that all citizens of the United States are possessed of the right to vote, and if its framers did not intend such a construction to be placed upon it, and if the States did not intend to ratify such Amendment, they now stand under the necessity of passing a supplementary Amendment providing that the rights of women citizens of the United States to vote may be denied by the States because they are women, which provision would not only include all white females, but also all colored females formerly in a " condition of servitude " to whom, under this Amendment, no State has the right to deny the right to vote.

This construction is made perfectly clear and applicable by Sec. 2 of Article VI. of the Constitution, which provides as follows : " This Constitution and the laws of the United States which shall be made in pursuance thereof   *   *   *   shall be the SUPREME LAW OF THE LAND   *   *   *   anything in the Constitution and laws of any State to the contrary notwithstanding." Therefore it is that in blending all those various parts and constructions together that we arrive at the conclusion that women as much as men are citizens of the United States, and that no State has any right to abridge the rights of citizens of the United States to vote, which, from the general construction of the Constitution, is guaranteed to every citizen, irrespective of sex or any other considered condition of inequality.

MARRIAGE AND DIVORCE.

CONSIDERATIONS FROM THE STANDPOINT OF COMMON SENSE — THE
MISAPPLICATION OF TERMS—WHO WOULD BE AFFECTED—WHAT IS
MARRIAGE?—WHAT IS DIVORCE?—THE COMMON CRY FOR LAWS TO
GUIDE EVERYBODY ELSE BUT OURSELVES.

When we observe the utterly senseless course adopted and followed
by some pretended advocates of political equality, and the self-assumed
pharisaical positions of others, we are at a loss to decide whether they
are not in a deal worse condition of servitude than that is from which
they profess to wish to rescue woman. They are determined that if
woman passes from Dan to Beer-sheba, she shall go by their route, and
that if she shall avail herself of any other easier, freer or less distant
route, that she shall be denied admission at the gates on her arrival.
They are like nearly all the religious sects that "preach" that there is
no way to heaven except by the way they point out; just as though
there are "sects in Heaven," and just as though God, the common pa-
rent of humanity, should care which way his children come home, so
that they come.

We do not believe there would be one-half the insane opposition
to political equality for all, were it not that it involves an equality which
to many is of much greater importance than *it* is. Political equality
cannot be granted to women, without their also obtaining sexual equality, a legitimate sequence, and just here is where all the hell-a-bell-loo

8

begins to show itself. If the enfranchised woman should still be compelled to remain the servile, docile, meekly-acquiescent, self-immolated and self-abnegative wife, there would be no difficulty about the voting. At the ballot-box is not where the shoe pinches, nor where the corn stings. It is at home where the husband, as in pre-historic times of anarchy, is the supreme ruler, that the little difficulty arises; he will not surrender this absolute power unless he is compelled.

But in spite of all opposition on the part of dominating man and submissive woman, the free of her sex are determined to obtain not only the political equality they seek, but also all other equalities which will naturally flow from its possession: having obtained which they will stand upon a broader platform of rights and see more distinctly what further legitimate, practical equality belongs to them.

Marriage, as consummated by present law, reduces the previously free, single woman to a condition of virtual slavery, in which she cannot proceed beyond certain boundaries without meeting the limitations of the contract which custom has prescribed. It is by no means an equal partnership. The wife has liberty within limits; the husband has license outside of all limits, and exercises it, too, whenever consistent with his inclinations. Political equality will soon settle this "little unpleasantness."

What is marriage? Is it a legal union between a male and female of the race of animals known as man; or does it have a wider and deeper significance? Are the "unions" between the males and females of the types of animals below man, marriages, or are they something else? Are the "unions" between the male and female species of plants, by which they reproduce and increase, marriages, or should they be designated by some other term? If these are marriages, who is there that will prepare some marriage law not in harmony with natural law, that shall compel each of these to forever remain mated, whether they would or no, and, by so being compelled, be enabled to ever remain respectable (?) members of their "society?"

Marriage, it is admitted by all, is some kind of a union of the opposite in sex; but, What constitutes it? Where is the point before reaching which is not marriage, and having passed which is marriage? Is it where two meet and realize for the first time they have found their other self; or is it where the priest or the squire reads a soulless formula over two who know no outreaching of souls and commingling of life's wishes, hopes and fears? Or does it require both these: first the marriage without the law, to be afterward made certain and lasting by the law? If the latter, does the marriage still continue if one of the terms which were necessary to first complete it should chance to depart? If, after marriage has transpired according to all requirements of law, and the law afterward declares a divorce, does that completely annul the marriage, supposing the primary terms of union still exist? Or, does marriage still continue if the first requirements cease to exist and the legal requirements do not cease to exist? Will they of the respectability (?) persuasion please give us an analysis of these things, so that we may be able to decide just what marriage consists of according to *their* " way to Heaven."

For our part, we are free to confess that we believe that any departure from nature's marriage law will be followed by disastrous consequences to all involved. We would not have it understood that we denounce all marriage laws; they may be very proper, and we are quite sure they are very harmless, and can very well be observed with perfect impunity by all who are truly possessed of the previous union. At this very point, however, begins the real question. Everybody who do not require a legal enforcement of law to *hold* them married want a legal law to hold everybody else married, whether such is their individual wishes or no. It is the same old story repeated. Everybody want laws to compel everybody else to do just as they want to do themselves. It is the same spirit that wishes every one to be guided by his standard. It is the same spirit that thinks self a great deal better than anybody else, and that everybody else must conform to the *dictum* of that self. It is the same spirit that says, " I do not require a law to punish theft, but my neighbor across the way I am fearful would steal from me if there were no such law."

" Oh! you horrid wretches, who would compel us all to become prostitutes, by annulling the law of marriage," came to us not long since from a person signing herself " A Reformer." We reply to all such: Oh, you horrid wretches who would compel us to prostitute ourselves, by compelling us through your marriage laws to remain the legal wives of those who have become detestable to us; who have time upon time forgotten their vows to us and have gone after strange women, and who, returning to us satiated with impurity, impose upon us the most frightful, the most horrible, the most loathsome results, which become not only an eternal curse to us but to our children. We tell you would-be "Reformers," that this is prostitution of the most damning kind, compared with which that commonly thus denominated is as white as snow and as harmless as the dove.

Suppose that all marriage laws were abolished, what would be the result? It is extremely doubtful if one-fourth of the present married would think of separating at all; and fully one-half of all who would separate would be extremely happy to return to their allegiance wiser and better within a short time. The final result would be simply this: that there would remain separate just those who by all rules of nature should not be allowed to live together as husband and wife. We conscientiously believe that the real—the natural, the religious, the philosophic, the scientific—want of the advancing, present age, is not a law to compel illy-assorted people to remain married to external appearances, but to separate them, so that the curses of their inharmonies may not be repeated in their children "even unto the fourth generation."

Among those who would permanently separate, were marriage laws abolished, there is a constant effort to obtain freedom. Most of them have established connections outside of their legal relations which they pursue whenever opportunity allows. Many of them resort to all manner of crime to be rid of their irksome bonds. They do not hesitate to perjure themselves even, to accomplish their desire; very many men actually have and support two families, sometimes more, spending most of their time with the natural marriage, and only what they are compelled to do for "appearance sake" with the legal marriage. No one who has not been extensively acquainted with society behind appearances could ever guess at the extentt to which bigamy is practised. There is nothing that is terrible enough to prevent two who are determined in these things from putting that determination into practice. The writer now knows a married woman who has six pressing suits for marriage from as many married men! What will be the result of such conditions? As was wisely remarked by one of our leading papers a few days since, "Much crime would be prevented were those who are determined not to remain husband and wife permitted to separate in quiet and peace."

The effect of a marriage law, which to all intents and purposes is irrevocable, is to make the subjects of it become careless and indifferent to each other, unless they are bound by a more powerful bond. They know they are safely bound together past all probability and nearly all possibility of separation. It becomes a matter of course that they are married for life, and all thought of those delicate attentions which are so heart-touching at all times from those we love, gradually passes away in indifference or becomes merged in the cares, perplexities and duties of life; whereas married life should never descend to the plane of duty, but should ever remain upon the plane of love's suggestions.

Very frequently married life is entered upon with very little thought of or care for the real conditions of union, because they do not fear that any trouble can come after the performance of the legal ceremony. Some even await that performance to afterward reveal their true purposes of fiendish complexion. Were it realized that marriages could only last while an approximate union of souls existed, there would be a deal more caution exhibited about entering that condition; there would be a deal more anxiety to know how much real union exists before taking on the final consummation.

It comes, therefore, that those who enter the marriage state most freely, are they who have little real attachment, their real object being to gain some other point rather than that of a perfect union; while those who give it the most consideration, regarding it as the gravest of life's movements, and who therefore think most of the true basis of marriage, are deterred from entering such engagements as are sufficient to practically ruin them if severed. These are of two classes: One consists of those men who fear that behind all the professions of love made them, motives of an entirely different character may rest, being the real mainspring which moves the person to profession, and which after marriage may develop themselves as the rule of conduct, and thus despoil a whole life of all the beauty and happiness to be obtained from marriage. The other consists of those women who, having given their hearts to men in whom past associations have wrought detrimental effect, fear that though married to them irrevocably they will not be reformed thereby, and that they, knowing they have their victims secure, will neither heed their vows nor their victims' entreaties or demands that the common usages of marriage shall be respected.

It is easily to be seen that in all cases where caution should be exercised and is not under present conditions, that it would be exercised to a very considerable extent were there no law binding bodies together whose hearts were found to be incompatible or which should become sundered; and these constitute a very considerable portion of all marriages; while in the cases recited above, the subjects having married and finding their fears too true, would not be virtually compelled to continue an existence of misery until death should dissolve the union.

It is not impossible, if this question of marriage could be entirely divested of all precedents of use, custom and other disabilities, and it could receive candid and unbiased discussion, and all its bearings could have unprejudiced analysis, that the public mind would soon learn that it has been clinging to a soulless idol, which has resulted in much of general misery, crime and ill to the race, having given for such no adequate return of increased virtue.

The present race of human beings is not altogether unregenerate. There are bad samples enough, heaven knows; but they are bad with the law, and they would be no worse without the law. Common experience is the great teacher, and it teaches in the matter of the union of the sexes that all the real happiness it is possible for humanity to know is in the pure and sacred relations of marriage, in which pure, holy and bright children spring into existence to gladden the prime of life and to lead with tender hand and firm the steps which descend the hill of life upon the other side, and who stand by your side upon the river's bank which soon will for a space separate you, and with one great, soul-inspiring love, realize that the bonds of flesh are but released that you may become still more closely united in spirit; and that of all the real misery there can be in life none is so terrible as that coming of marriage where the heart rests outside the limits of legal bonds.

There are a certain class of so-called or pretended advocates of equality for women, who seem to have but little just appreciation of the relations which exist between causes and effects; or, if they have any of this appreciation, they succeed in pretty effectually ignoring it. They take special pains to state, in the most emphatic and unmistakable language, that while they desire social equality with man, they do not want to vote, or to divest men of any of their superior political advantages which accrue to them from the exercise of that right which designates a republican government. The gist of their discourse is, "Give us everything else, but do not give us that by which we can have everything else by our own right." It is the same old story: "subjugated." Do these advocates expect that those having the power will render the sex justice, any more than the slave masters rendered their "property justice?" It would have been the height of folly for the negro to have cried out, "Give us justice!" when the law of the land recognized no justice for him. So, too, it is folly for woman to expect justice; she has first to take justice—that justice which is her inherent right with man to equality. Poetic fancy, and soft, sweet sentimentalities amount to but little in this matter-of-fact age, and when these speech-makers talk so submissively they of course gain the plaudits of men who fear that women are going to rebel against the superior family authority they have held unrebuked so long; they know that they now hold woman by the halter, which is long or short according to *their* inclination.

They see that the general tendency of all things which relate to the relative positions of men and women is to drift toward the obtaining of one rule of judgment and one rule for the execution of judgment. In this obtaining they know that their heretofore unquestioned authority, privileges and exclusive rights are to be extended, where they have thus far succeeded so well in excluding them, and that they must *share* rather than *possess* them.

Those who comprehend the real meaning of the Woman Move-ment are offering social equality as a compromise to those persons who refuse to labor in their interest. Social equality, forsooth! Will they please inform their next audiences which is the higher equality, political or social? If we understand this matter, we should say that social equality is the foundation of all equality, which having, all equality is possessed; perhaps our philosophy may be unsound, and that women may possess social equality and still be denied political equality. It, however, seems to us that the philosophy of these pseudo advocates of woman's equality teaches them an utter impossibility; for how can a people or any part of a people—in short, how can women enjoy social equality, unless they have a voice in making the laws that govern social life? Such a social equality as this would teach, our "fathers" pos-sessed when King George ruled them; such an equality as this would teach is now enjoyed by everybody who lives under an absolute mon-arch. Perhaps it may not be an absolute authority which persons ex-ercise over others whom they allow no voice in determining what that authority shall be; but we must confess that our dim senses cannot see it or feel it in that light. These players upon words want a great many laws altered. Do they expect to get this done by acknowledging their political nonentity and subserviency? This may be the theoretical way to reach that consummation, but the plain, practical, way would be to take hold of the matter themselves and assist in making the alterations. If woman is man's equal, let her demand the rights of an equal to assist in making her own laws: demand her rights, having obtained which, do with them as she will. These are the privileges of free men and equals. If she is not man's equal, Reformers (?) should cease ask-ing for social equality for her. But it is nearing the time wherein it must be settled what woman's status is, and what it is going to be. Men must either do one thing or the other; they must say women are equals and entitled to the privileges of equals; they must say that wo-men are not equals and are not entitled to the privileges of equals; or, that being equals, and entitled to the privileges of equality, that they

will not permit them to exercise such privileges because they are determined never to share their exercise, nor divide the patronage which
would naturally flow from such exercise. The point cannot be very
much longer ignored. The reason of the desire to continue woman in
political bondage must be made apparent, whatever the attempts of
female matrimonial bidders may be.

If woman's acquisition and practice of equality is going to break
up the family, as these lecturers prophesy, we should say it had better
be broken. If man cannot and will not submit to that practice, he had
better have no family, and thus practically place women upon the same
plane men occupy. As for the virtue side of the question, we confess
we hang our heads in veriest shame to hear our sex confess that all the
virtues they have is because they are bound by law to be virtuous, or
which means the same in other words, that if all marriage laws should
be abolished women would necessarily become prostitutes. Legal virtue has already become a cheap commodity, which is hawked nearly as
unblushingly by daylight as prostitution is under cover of night. Who
can tell how much prostitution there is which is shielded or hidden by
the *law?* Everybody who knows anything knows it is alarming, not
to say a great deal worse. If there are no virtuous wives nor virtuous
husbands, except those made so by law, we would say, God help such
virtue! for, modifying scripture to suit the times, those who look upon
others to lust after them have already committed adultery in their own
hearts   No! a thousand times, no!   Virtue and every other noble
quality is of the heart, and he or she who possesses it, does so whether
there is law or not, and should such be entirely removed from the
force of law, it would not follow that they must necessarily "advance
or retreat to license." We have more faith than this in human nature
as a whole ; at the same time we aver.that those who would not be virtuous *without* a compelling law, *will* not with one.

But all that this school of speakers and writers of the female sex say
sounds exceedingly nice, and we have no doubt that "The Mr. Temples of society, who want wives moulded to their requirements," will
thank them continuously, and *encore* them as frequently as opportunity
offers, for doing their battles for them, and set them all down as the
veriest pinks of womanly—wifely—perfection. The argument they
make it possible for men to urge against equality is the strongest and
the only real one there is : that women themselves don't want to vote.
This very specious argument is heralded as sufficient and convincing,
though in reality there is so little basis to it that it will stand analysis

no better than a sieve will hold water. Exceptional cases exist where women have stated that they do not desire the elective franchise; perhaps one in every hundred—not more—women have so expressed themselves. Do they affect to speak for the other ninety-nine? It may be replied that the same argument may be applied to the other side of the question, and that those who advocate suffrage for women are in equal disproportion to the total of women. And this brings us to the point, and the point is this: The advocates of equal suffrage advocate it upon the general principles of equality, and affirm that women being equal to men in all general privileges, that it is their right to exercise the right of suffrage which belongs to every American citizen of legal age who has not forfeited it by crime. Whether every woman, one-half, one-tenth, or one-hundredth part of women, avail themselves of the right or not is perfectly immaterial. The right exists, and it is theirs to choose whether they shall use it or not; which position is somewhat different, we take it, from that which denies the exercise of an existing right. One is freedom; the other is tyranny. And that is just the difference. With you who retort upon us with this question, we propose you take this consideration home, and when next you speak against extending suffrage to women, do not forget that your opponents deal with principles of freedom while you deal with the assumptions of tyranny.

We would, therefore, venture to suggest that before entering the arena for the discussion of reforms based on principles, these persons should study the relations of political and social equality, which will undoubtedly teach them, as everybody else is taught, that if a wrong is to be remedied, the direct way to right that wrong is to go to the root of the matter at once, and the root of the inequalities which flourish between man and woman lies in the lack of possession and exercise of social equality. Political equality may be possessed and social equality still be lacking; but with the possession of social equality all equality is gained. If they do not do this they will lay themselves liable to be set down as the representatives of that very large class of women who prefer to remain under the dominion and support of man rather than to take on themselves the responsibilities and duties of freedom and a noble independence and self-reliance. So that it comes down to this at last: that it is maintenance that women want who "don't want to vote," instead of freedom, which others are seeking. If this freedom should chance to change the forms of relationship between the sexes it will do nothing more serious than to give equality in them. The re-

lations themselves can never be done away with.   Hence we conclude
that marriage and divorce in the abstract are meaningless terms, and
that at best they are only names for continually changing forms, which
always have changed and always will change, until the time when it
will be possible for "Unions" to exist in their greatest perfection,
whether the form continues or not.

CHILDREN.

A series of papers, relating specifically to women, cannot well be closed without something being said relative to their offspring. We say their offspring, because it is they who, by nature, are appointed to the holy mission of motherhood, and who, by this mission, are directly charged with the care of the embryotic life, upon which so much of future good or ill to it depends. It is during this brief period that the initials of character are stamped upon the receptive, incipient mentality, which, expanding as it grows, first into childhood and on to manhood or womanhood, reveals the true secrets of its nature.

The rights of children, then, as individuals, begin while yet they are in the fœtal life, and it is to this consideration that attention is most required to be called, for here lies the cause of a great deal more of the conditions of life than we have been taught to think. Children do not come into existence by any will or consent of their own. With their origin they have nothing to do, but in after life they take upon themselves individual responsibility, and thus become liable for action which perhaps was predetermined by circumstances which occurred long prior to their assuming personal responsibility. In all those years before individual responsibility and discretion, which are by common consent accorded to youth, children are virtually the dependencies of their parents, subject to their government, which may be either wise or mischievous, and is as often the latter as the former. But, having arrived at the proper age, they step into the world upon an equality of footing with others previously arrived. At this time they are the result of the care which has been bestowed upon them from the time of conception, and whether they are delivered over to the world in such condition as to promise to be useful members of its society, or whether they go into it to prove a constant annoyance and curse to it, seems to be a matter which cannot be made into such shape of personal responsibility as to make it a subject of their own determining. At this period they find themselves possessed of a body and a partially developed mind, in the union of which a harmonious disposition and character may have resulted ; respectively, they are possessed of all shades of disposition and character, from the angelic down to the most demoniacal ; but all these are held accountable to the same laws ; are expected to govern themselves by the same formula of associative justice, and are compelled by the power of public opinion to subscribe to the same general customs.

This system of unequal justice is the legitimate result of the doctrine of free will, which says, in practice, that a devil who has been produced and cast upon the world by some of its members, is expected to act under all circumstances and changes just as well and justly as a perfect man does. That he will or can do so everybody knows is impossible. All are obliged to meet the world and all its variety of circumstance and change with the characteristics with which they have been clothed, and which they had no choice in selecting. How inconsistent it is to suppose that, with so great diversity, which is so extensive that there can, by no possibility, be two who so nearly resemble each other as to be mistaken for each other, there can be unity of action, or the same rule of compliance to the requirements of society on the part of all its members. Thus when all things which go to make up society are analyzed and formulated, it comes out that society holds its individual members responsible for deeds which it is itself indirectly the cause of, and therefore responsible for.

Have not the offending members of society been generated, born and grown under its own prescribed rules, which they had no choice of or escape from? and yet they are made the responsible parties. It is a scientifically demonstrated fact that the mind of every individual member of society is the result of a continuous series of impressions, which are the product of it as a community and which are continually being received from it by their senses and by them transmitted to, and taken up by consciousness, which thus becomes the individuality of the person. If any one doubt this, let him listen to what Prof. J. W. Draper, Presi-

dent of the New York University, Medical College, says upon this subject. He certainly is authority which none will dispute without consideration, however quickly they might attempt to gainsay the simple
assertion of others. This subject is worthy of the most serious attention which can be bestowed upon it, for it is the point which determines
where the real responsibility of individual action rests, as well as the
point which, properly and legitimately considered, should govern all
attempts at reform in the present condition of society. In a lecture delivered Prof. Draper says as follows ·

"There are successive phases   *   *   *   in the early action of the mind. As soon as the senses are in working order   *   *
a process of collecting facts is commenced. These are at first of the
most homely kind, but the sphere from which they are gathered is extended by degrees. We may, therefore, consider that this collecting of
facts is the earliest indication of the action of the brain, and it is an
operation which, with more or less activity, continues through life.   *
*   *   Soon a second characteristic appears—the learning of the
relationship of the facts thus acquired to one another.   *   *   *
This stage has been sometimes spoken of as the dawn of the reasoning
faculty. A third characteristic of almost contemporaneous appearance
may be remarked—it is the putting to use facts that have been acquired
and the relationships that have been determined. *   *   *   Now
this triple natural process   *   *   *   must be the basis of any
right system of instruction." It appears, then, that contact and constant
intercourse with external manifestations is not only necessary for the
production of thought and its collaterals, but that to retain the consciousness which makes thought possible such manifestations must be
continuously impressed upon the individual. This seems to be conclu-
sive that mind is the result of the experiences of the manifestations of
power.

Without these experiences children would grow up simply idiotic.
The "Professor" says, emphatically, that a recognition of this process
must be the basis for any right system of instruction. Nor is it to be
understood that he would make the application of this simply to intellectual education. It applies with equal force to all kinds and relations
of education; or, to state the proposition comprehensively, the education of children should consist in surrounding them by such circumstances and facts as will produce upon them those effects which will
tend to develop them toward our highest idea of perfect men and women. When this system shall have been introduced and made general,
education will have attained to its proper sphere. How imperfect all
our present methods are need scarcely be mentioned. It is patent to

all who have candor sufficient to allow them to admit it, that perfection has not yet been gained in any of our systems and forms of instruction. A great deal has been said and is being done in the matter of reforming them, but we fear very little of it is based on Professor Draper's propositions.

The chief difficulty about all these things is that their direction has been left to, or assumed by, the professors of religion rather than by scientists with whom religionists have, until quite recently, been at a dead lock, and still remain at great divergence from, in regard to these matters. Science is eminently progressive; religion is as eminently conservative. Science, in its analysis of the facts of the age, comes in direct conflict with the authoritative theories of religious sects, whose advocates having the possession of the general system of common education, are not inclined to admit it to the platform of scientific deduction. Happily, these things are now undergoing rapid change, and they who once taught that the world was created out of nothing in six days and nights, of twenty-four hours each, have given way to the demonstrations of geology, and are forced to admit that their previous belief was founded in an allegory.

The ice which has held firm so long, being broken, is gradually though surely disappearing, and the day is not far distant when all things will be submitted to the test of demonstration, and everything which will not stand it will be discarded as good for nothing except to deceive. In nothing is this needed so much as in determining what education should consist of, so as to furnish to the world the best samples of physical, mental and moral excellence combined. Neither of these departments can be neglected ; they must all be merged together into one system, and that must be guided by the deductions to be derived from the previously stated proposition.

The common practice of the world, in all things which it desires to modify or remedy, is to begin at the extreme, where the effects are found, and from them to work backward toward the beginning. The whole course of the world regarding crime has been to punish rather than to prevent it; to work with the effects of education—for it comes down to that at last—rather than to perfect the system of education. And if we begin the statement by saying that education commences almost at the period of conception and extends until men and women take control of themselves, we shall have been only comprehensive; enough to have included that portion of life for which the community— society—is strictly responsible. And there is no escape from this conclusion. What the man or woman is at the time they become recognized citizens, society makes them. They are its production as much as the apple is the production of the tree. If the apple is a bad apple it is not its fault; that lies in the tree. If men and women are bad men and women when they arrive at legal age, it is not their fault but it is the fault of society in which they are born, raised and educated.

No. II.

Having in a previous number come to the deliberate conclusion that society is responsible for the character of the children which it rears to become constituent, responsible members of itself, it now becomes necessary to examine the conditions and circumstances through which they are compelled to attain to their responsibility, and to decide which, if any part thereof, is not in keeping with the logic of responsibility after majority.

In making this examination there can be no departure from the most inflexible applications of principles allowed. The clear, the full, the broadest generalizations and specializations must be maintained, while in immediate practice such approaches to the same will be advocated as are possible in present conditions.

It is the worst failing—it has always been the worst failing—of all advocates of reform based in principles, that they can see nothing but an immediate abandonment of all present customs and the full and complete adoption of all the legitimate deductions of these principles, which, though they may be abstractly correct and logically unavoidable, are too widely separated from prevailing practices to admit of an instant transfer from the old to the new. The practical reformers are they who, while keeping a steadfast hold of the full and broadest application of principles, instead of endeavoring to compel society to gain this by one leap, guide it toward it gradually. To·society the process may be almost imperceptible or so nearly so that on arriving at the desired point it will not be conscious of the advance it has made. It is not without reason that the world calls all reformers in new fields "impracticables," and it is for just the reason which we have endeavored to point out.

Particular stress is laid upon this, that our own course may not be deemed inconsistent. While we shall advocate the extent of all that should be, regarding the preparation of children to become active and useful members of society, we would have it distinctly understood that its practice must be reached by degrees. If we are hungry and cannot get a whole loaf of bread, it would be most foolish to starve when the half of it could have been had and our craving thus partially satisfied. So, too, is it with reform. If all that the keenest analysis teaches cannot be arrived at immediately, the practice of a part should satisfy for the time.

It is scientifically true that the life which develops into the individual life never begins. That is to say, there is no time in which it can be said life begins where there was no life. The structural unit of nucleated protoplasm, which forms the centre around which aggregation proceeds, contains a pulsating life before it takes up this process. As the character of the herve stimula which this is possessed of and which sustains this evidence of life must depend upon the source from which it proceeds, it is first of all important that the condition of this source should be favorable to the new organism which it is to furnish the nucleus of. In other words, and plainly, the condition of the parents at the time of conception, should be made a matter of prime importance, so that the life principle with which the new organism is to begin its growth should be of the highest order.

There are various evidences which have been collected from time to time by the medical profession which leave no doubt as to the importance of beginning life according to the strictest requirements or harmony.

Cases of partial and total idiocy have been traced to the beastly inebriation of the parents at and previous to the time of conception. On the other extreme, some of the brightest intellects and the most noble and loveable characters the world ever produced owed their happy condition to the peculiarly happy circumstances under which they began life, much of the after portion of the growing process of which having been under unfavorable circumstances. Many ' mothers can trace the irritable and nervously-disagreeable condition of their children to their own condition at this time. It must therefore be allowed that the condition under which every child is generated has an important bearing upon the whole future life.

How important it is, then, that proper consideration should govern in this the beginning of life. It is surely a matter of sufficient moment to be reduced to a strictly scientific basis.

We are aware that these subjects are not only avoided, but are almost unanimously ignored by society; also, that society pretends to blush at the mention of them ; and well it may blush, for the abortions of nature which it is continually turning upon the world to be its pests, its devils, its damnation and their own worst enemies, are sufficiently hideous to make all humanity blush with well-founded shame. We have no doubt that the noble dames of society, the mincing, supercilious, affected graduates of those hot-houses of female depravity—boarding-schools—with all the ignorant and bigoted, will hold up their hands in holy horror to think that women should so degrade themselves as to attempt to discuss these subjects. But the time must come wherein they will not only be discussed, but must be understood and practiced according to the understanding—when a full knowledge of what pertains to conception, fœtal life, birth and growth to full manhood and womanhood, will be an important part of every child's education.

Virtue nor modesty does not consist in the avoidance, the ignoring, or ignorance of these most important things ; but true virtue, true modesty and true general worth, consist, in part at least, of a complete knowledge and practice of them. It is full time that we have done with all the sham modesty and affected virtue with which humanity has been cursed already too long and unnecessarily. As has been said before, reformers are all working at the wrong end of the matter, foolishly, blindly, uselessly ; they attempt to control effects, not to remedy causes. Such reformers never have and never will accomplish much except to set others thinking.

It is required in this subject of the life of children, that we begin at the very root of the matter ; and that lies in the condition of persons, about to become parents. The mere matter of the observance of formula and customs of society is not, by one thousandth part, as important as that is which shall decide the character of a future individualized human being. And just to this point, as we have said before, is where the Woman Question leads. It is the important question of the age, and it will rise to be thus acknowledged. All present humanity has a direct interest in it ; and all future humanity demands of the present its right to the best life which it is possible to have under the best arrangement of present circumstances which can be formulated. And there are those who will not permit that their rights be much longer ignored. There will be " John the Baptists " preaching in the wilderness, " Prepare ye the way," and humanity must and will heed them. Such is the prophecy of the present ; and the present will do well to listen to its teachings.

The holy mission of fathers and mothers is the most sacred of all earthly duties, and to be able to faithfully and perfectly perform them, in a full knowledge of their importance, should be the ambition of every human being. Very much of the fashionable external nonsense, which forms so great a part of young ladies' education, might well be dispensed with, and they, instead, be instructed in their mission as the artists of humanity; artists not merely in form and feature, but in that diviner sense of intellect and soul.

No. III.

We have often wondered that, among all the medical authorities, there have not been more who devoted some part of their profuse writings to the ante-natal care and treatment of children. No more important addition could be made to our system of social economy, nor to our pathological literature, than a strictly scientific analysis of fœtal life for popular and familiar circulation. While so much has been said and written—much of which, to be sure, is very foolish and unprofitable—regarding children's care and treatment after birth, that part of their life previously has been entirely ignored. It would be just as proper to ignore their life after birth until some still future period, say three, five or seven years of age, as to do so previously.

To lay a good foundation for a good life, it is required that the proper care should be bestowed upon it from its very point of beginning. The same rule should apply and govern, which applies and governs in all similar matters outside of and below the most important of them all. Even the tiller of the soil exercises special care and his best wisdom in the matter of preparation for the future harvest. He knows, from oft-repeated experience, how important it is, first of all, to have the very best seed, of the very best variety, to plant. For this he selects the choicest and most perfect of his preceding crop, or purchases from others who have better than he. He knows that seed thus selected, planted side by side with unselected seed, and receiving no more care, will yield not only larger harvests but also that they will be of choice quality.

Having obtained the best seed possible, his next step is to have the ground properly prepared, into which, at just the proper season, he deposits it. All these introductory and preparatory measures of care and study are a part of the process by which our fruits, grains and vegetables have been brought to their present state of perfection. Everybody knows that fruits and vegetables which grow wild and are poisonous, are oftentimes capable of being brought, by cultivation, to be useful and delicious articles of diet. Everybody knows that it has been only by the strictest study and care that our most celebrated breeds of horses and other stocks of domesticated animals have been obtained. Everybody knows that deep scientific research is constantly being made regarding almost every department of production, and that those engaged in the respective departments, eagerly seek and systematically apply every new fact which science makes clear. And it is, scientifically, an admitted fact, that the future character of what is to be produced can be very nearly, if not absolutely, determined by those who have charge of the process through which it is to be produced. Even the color which the herdsman desires for his cattle can be literally obtained; and what is true regarding color is just as broadly true regarding all other indices of individuality.

Notwithstanding all these accepted facts which are coming to be the rules and guides of all people, when we approach the subject of making the same rules and guides so general in their application as to include children, the world stands aghast, and, with one united effort, frowns it down.

Nobody denies the importance of the subject, but those who will speak at all argue that it is one of those things which the common mind is not prepared to meet. Not prepared to meet! And the whole Christian world has been preaching regeneration these eighteen hundred years! which they tell us is the one thing necessary. All the importance claimed for regeneration we willingly admit; all badly produced persons require regeneration; but as to it being the main thing, we beg to demur. If regeneration is an important matter, generation is still more so. It is to the consideration of this scientific fact, as demonstrated and practiced by the human, in all departments of nature below, that the human must come, and acknowledge itself a proper subject of. Just so far as science can demonstrate and humanity will put its demonstrations to practice, just so far will the necessity for regeneration be done away.

It is too true that the courage to face this question has always been wanting, and that when it is attempted, all society pretends to be outraged by it. Are Human Beings, then, to always be considered of so much less importance than the very things they make subservient to them, that they should forever be left to come into this world's exist-

ence as individuals at random?   We know the obloquy that has fallen
upon all who have ever attempted to hold the mirror so that society
would be obliged to contemplate itself; but, notwithstanding all this,
we feel there is not a more noble object to which we can turn.   We have
deliberately considered all the bearings of this matter, and have as deliberately determined to stand by the flag we have reared so long as we
shall have life and strength to do so.   We have thrown to the world—
" Children : their Rights, Privileges and True Relations to Society," and
,we shall maintain it argumentatively, if possible; defiantly, if need be,
against all opposition, let it come from whence it may, or let its character be what it may.   Argument we know we shall not have to encounter.   Scientific hindrances we know we shall not find in our path. Common Sense we know will offer no word of reproof. We shall, however,
encounter hoary-headed bigotry, blind intolerance and fossilized authority—and we are prepared.

It is laid down as an undeniable proposition, that the Human Race
can never even approximate to perfection until all the means which
men make use of to produce perfect things are also made use of in their
own production.   Let those who decry this proposition turn to their
so-much-revered Bible and read—" Ye cannot gather figs of thorns nor
grapes from thistles "—and learn wisdom therefrom.   It must be remembered how great an " infidel " was he who first demonstrated Arterial
and Veinous circulation, which has come to be of the greatest importance in diagnosing diseases.   It has generally been proven true, that
those things which have resulted in the greatest benefit to humanity,
met with the most blind and insane opposition in their first struggles for
recognition.   If this subject of children is to be judged by this rule, it
is to develop into greater importance than any which has yet occupied
the human mind.   Were the inquisition, the rack, the stake possible in
this age of the world, its advocates would be at their mercy, for they
would be used unmercifully.

But, it is asked by those who have somewhat recovered from the
first shock of the proposition that the propagation of the human species
should be reduced to rules, How can this be done?   It cannot be done
immediately to the fullest extent, but the recognition of its importance
can be forced upon humanity, and the practice of its evident deductions
can be attained by degrees.   Once let it become divested of this absurd
idea of "impropriety," and humanity will begin to practice its teachings.   It is only required that reason be exalted to its proper place and
influence, and analogies, with which nature abounds, will become the

great teachers. Almost everything which is required to be known and practiced to produce healthy, happy and good children in every sense of that word, is already known and practiced in every other kind of reproduction.

The great difficulty with which we shall be met at every step is, that it is nearly impossible to make people realize that their lives here are for any other or higher purpose than for each of them to acquire for him or herself the greatest amount of *personal,* and consequently selfish, gratification. They cannot yet sufficiently realize that each individual is made one of the means by which the whole of humanity is advanced. They cannot yet be brought to reduce to practice what all will admit, that he or she is the greatest man or woman who does the most for humanity; nor have they yet anything more than an undefined belief that in doing the most for humanity, they do most for themselves. Yet this has been the logic of the doctrine of Christianity nearly two thousand years.

The teachings of Christianity are all well; they have been taught persistently. But we have now arrived at that practical age of the world which demands adequate results as proofs of the validity of assumed positions. The Apostles taught that "certain signs" should follow those who believed. Do these signs exist within the heart of the professedly sole representatives of true Christianity? By their fruits shall ye know them. We do know them by their fruits, which are not so perfect as to warrant the conclusion that humanity has yet passed from being "professors" into being "possessors." That this process is not farther advanced is, because the laborers in "the vineyard" are endeavoring to compel scraggy, scranny, ill-formed, ill-tempered sources to produce perfected fruit.

Human life may be compared to a military campaign, in which no amount of valiancy and good generalship can overcome the defects of an imperfect organization of the "body"—army—with which it is to be made. We may as consistently expect a badly organized army to make a good military champaign as to expect a badly organized child to make a good social campaign. To this the very beginning of organization, should all reformers turn who expect to produce any beneficial results, which shall be ultimate and lasting, and which shall mark the perfecting process of humanity.

No. IV.

If there is one thing in the whole round of individualized life which should be considered more important than any other, or even all the rest, it is the individualized existence of the human. If life be analyzed with the view to discover the ultimate purposes of the creation as represented by the part this planet fills in the solar system, it will be found that no higher evolution is posssible than that of mind, as individualized in the human.

Human mind consists of all grades of comprehensiveness and refinement, from the mere brutal to the angelic. The best aim a human being can entertain is to attain the highest perfection in intellect, morals and in spirituality. The best endowment a human being can have is such an organization as will admit of and render easy the acquisition and devolvement of these beauties of the inner life. Mere physical beauty and perfection, although a thing more to be desired than all other material things, cannot compare with that richer endowment of interior beauty. A beautiful fiend is the most sorrowful sight the world can contemplate; next to which is an angelic soul resident in a material deformity.

Material evolutioh has ultimated in the production of the human form, and it is made male and female, not by mere chance, but that further, greater and nobler ends may be gained. These ends are arrived at through the union of the sexes and by their reproducing their kind. The grandest purpose of human life, then, must be the reproduction of the most perfect specimens of its kind, and this is the logical deduction to which all sensible, reasoning persons must arrive. If this be so, then nothing should be held so important as a perfect understanding of the laws which control all things which are involved in the processes of nature relating to reproduction.

Instead of this being a subject to be tabooed, ignored or ridiculed, it should be raised to the one standing first in importance over all other subjects for general discussion, both verbal and written. The entire practice of the world is in direct opposition to this proposition. Reproduction, instead of being made the chief aim of life, is about the only part of it which is left to "luck and chance." Teach, read, study everything else, but this is too delicate a subject to admit attention; everybody should show their wisdom, sense and breeding by a studied avoidance of it, has been and still is the practice. Thanks to the spirit of progress which is abroad in the world, this stupidity, this ignorance, this vulgarity, aye, this brutality, is declining, and the age of reason and common sense is advancing to occupy their place. Nevertheless, it is ground which must yet be approached carefully and surveyed but partially, in order to insure countenance from those who should give it attention. And this is why we have endeavored to show the importance and the necessity of it at such length.

The New York *Tribune* asserts that the cause of half the vice among us is the ignorance of parents of the fact that certain nervous and cerebral diseases transmitted from themselves tend to make of their children from their birth criminals or drunkards, and that only incessant and skilful care can avert the danger. The editor then goes on to philosophize in this way:

"A man may drink moderately but steadily all his life, with no apparent harm to himself, but his daughters become nervous wrecks, his sons epileptics, libertines, or incurable drunkards, the hereditary tendency to crime having its pathology and unvaried laws, precisely as scrofula, consumption, or any other purely physical disease. These are stale truths to medical men, but the majority of parents, even those of average intelligence, are either ignorant or wickedly regardless of them. There will be chance of ridding our jails and almshouses of half their tenants when our people are taught to treat drunkenness as a disease of the stomach and blood as well as of the soul, to meet it with common sense and a physician, as well as with threats of eternal damnation, and to remove gin-shops and gin-sellers for the same reason that they would stagnant ponds or uncleaned sewers. Another fatal mistake is pointed out in the training of children—the system of cramming, hot-house forcing of their brains, induced partly by the unhealthy, feverish ambition and struggle that mark every phase of our society, and partly for the short time allowed for education. The simplest physical laws that regulate the use and abuse of the brain are utterly disregarded by educated parents. To gratify a mother's silly vanity during a boy's school days, many a man is made incompetent and useless. If the boy show any sign of unnatural ambition or power, instead of regarding it as a symptom of an unhealthy condition of the blood vessels or other cerebral disease, and treating it accordingly, it is accepted as an evidence of genius, and the inflamed brain is taxed to the uttermost, until it gives way exhausted."

When a paper, which so religiously ostracizes so much which is involved in the principles of general reform, as the *Tribune* does, comes so near to the "root of the matter," it may be seriously considered whether the time has not arrived in which to speak directly to the point. If these effects follow from the causes cited, what is the remedy? All who will stop a moment and calmly consider the situation will agree with the *Tribune*, and go still further to say that many other vices not mentioned by it are attributable to the same sources. The question for the reformer, then, is not how much of the so-called evil of the world has its origin behind the individual enacting it, but the vital question is: How shall this damnation be made to cease?

One thing is certain, that if parents continue to produce children under these circumstances the effects will continue. The remedy, then, is twofold : first, and mainly, to prevent, as much as possible, the union of persons addicted to these false practices ; second, to endeavor to reform those who are united.

A positive assertion is here made. No two persons have the right to produce a human life and irremediably entail upon it such a load of physical and mental hell as the *Tribune* cites ; and if they do they should be held accountable to society for the evils resulting therefrom. It is the merest sham of justice to punish the drunkard for the sins of his or her parents. It is the most superficial nonsense and the purest malice to curse the bad fruit which grows in your orchard because you do not take care of the trees ; but it is not more so than it is to curse and punish children for the crime of their parents. From whatever attitude this question is viewed it cannot fail to become obvious that society is working at the wrong end of the dilemma to regenerate the world. Regeneration must continue indefinitely. But give proper attention to generation and the end is half accomplished from that time.

We come back, then, to the original proposition, that society is itself directly accountable for the ills with which it is affected, and that it should be held accountable to the children it produces and turns loose into itself rather than that they should be made accountable to society for their shortcomings. And this is the inevitable logic of common sense, and is supported by the analysis of all facts.

No. V.

We are aware that the proposition with which the last article closed is a novel one, but from the premises no other conclusion can be reached. And if such be the true responsibilities of the situation, it necessarily follows that society should make it one of its first and most important duties to itself as a whole, to compel its constituent parts to a due regard for the laws of reproduction.

Marriage or the union of the sexes is a natural condition of the human race to which its sex representatives legitimately tend. The result to society of marriage is addition to its numbers. The result to the contracting parties is just the happiness or the misery which they extract from their union. Whatever relations they may sustain to the children they produce, those which society as a whole sustains to them are broader and more comprehensive. The parents are but parts of society, and their children are nothing less, so that while they, by present social systems, are for a long time left to the special control and guardianship of their parents, it can be considered only as in trust for society.

The relations which should be considered as the foundation of society are those which exist between society and marriage in its special function of reproduction, which thus far has been utterly ignored. When two are about to form a marriage union, does society in its legitimate functions of promoting and protecting the public welfare ever stop to ask what the character of the results of the union are likely to be? Instead of this most proper question entering into the consideration, the only one that has been thought of is is: How shall these two be compelled to live out the remainder of their natural lives together, utterly regardless of the higher thought of the children resulting from it? Such has been and is the superficiality of society, and consequently in its heart and nerve to-day it is degenerated and corrupt, though to external appearances it is proud and gay.

But, says the objector, would you cripple individual freedom by imposing any restraints regarding the union of the sexes? We answer that individual freedom which interferes with the good of the public is not freedom but tyranny. Every living individual is possessed of the inalienable right to freedom within the limits of his or her sphere, but that freedom cannot encroach upon the freedom of any other individual possessing the same right, nor upon that of the sum of individuals as represented by society. Just at this point is where the great mistake is always made: the failure is ever made to distinguish between individual and collective rights and wrongs, between society as the total of individuals and the individuals themselves. The rights of the former are so much the more superior to those of the latter, as it is greater in the number of individuals composing it. Under this poposition, which

lies at the root of all government, society not only has the right to prescribe all necessary laws by which to govern its members, but it is its
duty both to itself as a body and to every individual member to do so.
Anything in the individual which produces deleterious effects upon society it has the right to constrain, but beyond this limit no government
has any right to proceed.

It may be laid down as as an undeniable and legitimate duty of
society through its established government to debar, if possible, the production of such children as prove the pests and curse of it, which action, in its results, the blindest and dumbest can see must be beneficial
to all parties involved, to society as a whole, and to those debarred from
inflicting upon it the coming damnation.

Were these matters understood, were they made a part and parcel
of every child's education, there would be but little, if any, disposition
on the part of individuals to proceed contrary to the limits of these deductions. It may be considered as certain that no woman would consent to bear children by an habitual drunkard, did she know that it
would legitimately follow that such children must be idiotic, insane or
the subjects of epilepsy; and if she would she should be prevented.
It may not be true that such dire results often follow, but many others,
only less terrible, surely do in every such case.

It is a well-established fact among the medical profession that nearly,
if not quite, all the consumption which hurries so many victims through
life has its source in hereditary syphilitic taint, which, for delicacy,
has been christened scrofula. Now what business or right has a man
or woman, who knows that his or her system is loaded with this infer-
nal poison, to become the propagator of the species? It requires but a
moment of just consideration to determine between the individual's
rights and those of society in this instance. The same is equally true
of all other diseases and damnations which can be transmitted, and not
more of those which pertain to the purely physical than of those which
relate to the mental and the moral. It thus must come to be a conceded
fact that the rights of society are superior in every sense to those of the
individuals composing it. When the world shall begin to act upon this
deduction it will have commenced a course of advancement which will
never be intermixed with retreats.

Education for all in matters which refer to these vital points should
be one of the first steps to be taken by society. They have been foolishly and criminally ignored upon the false premises that to instruct
children in them would be to lead them into unfortunate conditions,

whereas the very reverse is the truth. The same principle should and does hold true in this regard that does in all which have been demonstrated. If there are dangers to be avoided, the very best way to prepare children to avoid them is to give them a perfect understanding of what they are. In knowledge there is always safety. In ignorance there is always danger.

Let these truths be adopted in the education of children, regarding their duties as the future parents of society, and one-half the ills with which society is inflicted would soon disappear. No person would think of setting their children to carry on a business of which they had no knowledge, but in this, the most vital of all things—the production of their kind—all possible knowledge is withheld. As well might it be expected that an ignorant foot-pad should be able to construct a perfect locomotive as that ignorant parents should be able to produce perfect children; and society must come to this conclusion before much progress can be possible in purifying the races.

Notwithstanding all the very bad material which exists out of which future generations will be constructed, those generations will be very much improved by a judicious culture of the bad we have—just as superior stocks of animals, better fruits and vegetables, and more perfectly perfumed flowers are produced from inferior sources. It is the knowledge which shall bring to men and women the comprehension of these things which is needed; with it very few bad results would follow, even from the bad we have.

It requires but to be mentioned to show the ridiculousness, the absurdity, to say nothing all about the lying part of the matter, of endeavoring to mislead children by such falsehoods as that "the doctor brought mamma a baby last night." To such an extent has this ignorance prevailed that young women have actually been married without knowing anything about the process of reproduction If such things are not criminal it is hard to name anything which is. Thanks to a great deal which is obtained nowadays in spite of parents and teachers, not many women enter the marriage state without some knowledge of what they are to be the subjects of.

If our houses of prostitution were searched and their inmates questioned, none would be found there whose mothers had the good sense to teach them the objects and functions of their sexual systems. It is the ignorance of these things which prepares the subjects who fill the blotches upon the fair face of humanity, which scatter their blighting poisons among its sons and daughters. In the name of a common humanity, then, and as a duty we owe it, we demand that these curses be banished by a sensible and judicious system of common education. There is a law common to all nature by which those things that are best adapted to each other are brought and held together. If it be analogically applied, there will be found a chemistry of the social, intellectual and moral sentiments as well as of the material elements, which only requires to have free action to produce equally good comparative results. Education should include a perfect knowledge of this part of general chemistry, so that compatibles may be at once apparent to all people of both sexes. Open the fountains of knowledge so that all may drink of the waters of a true life.

<hr />

No. VI.

If "knowledge is power," ignorance must be weakness; hence it is that we insist that knowledge is a matter of primary importance regarding the relations of the sexes. All the legislation and provision of the past has been short-sighted, having been entirely directed to maintaining relations once entered upon during life, just as though these relations begun and ended within themselves, and never giving the results of these relations even the first thought except to keep them as ignorant as possible during their growth of the processes of nature by which they are.

With knowledge upon these matters entering into circumstances which control marriages, something more than mere personal and temporary considerations would assume the determining position. People would, in the first place, never think of contracting sexual alliances with those through whom they should have any cause to suspect that their offsprings would be curses to them and society; and, in the second place, having given such alliances consideration, reason would prevail, and, in the majority of instances, prevent their consummation. There are various cases, however, in which, with all the precaution which knowledge would engender, persons would find themselves allied before discovering causes which should absolutely deter them from continuing the union. This we are aware touches the question of marriage law, which has been so fully treated upon elsewhere, but it is a point to which legislators have never given any weight or thought whatever, and it therefore demands attention. If marriage is for any other purpose than simply the binding together of two individuals for the mere sake of having them bound, then these purposes should have a modifying power over the union itself. If people—sensible people— set about to accomplish any purpose, they exert their best talent to adapting the means to the end in view ; they do not blindly set about it without considering what the results of certain steps would be ; in other words, they sit down and " count the cost" and see if their means will compass the ends.

As we have said before, no two have any right to contract an alliance by which children shall result to curse the world. Children are the results—the natural results—of these alliances, and as they are the end to be attained by the alliance, they should be the chief consid- eration to determine it. People drink to quench their thirst ; but they do not necessarily seize upon the first liquid they come upon and make use of it, regardless of the effect it will produce. It is one of the sim- plest rules of life which we are insisting upon, and yet people have never discovered that it conld apply to marriage. The reason why this has not been discovered is because pure selfishness has controlled with ab- solute sway.

The time has come, however, wherein something more than present personal considerations must assume their true determining positions regarding marriage ; in which either sex must ask the question and an- swer-it before action, What shall I contribute to humanity if I do this ? To this condition education will lead in these matters as surely as it does in all others. Then let us have a judicious system of education relating to the laws which govern reproduction, nor let it be longer absurdly held that there is danger in it to the young who have arrived at matu- rity in function.

The same rule which applies in all other things also does in this. Familiarity with everything relating to it removes all danger of injury or of pernicious results flowing from it. To make use of an illustration in the direct line in which this matter has been considered by society, and which invests all secrets with a peculiar fascination for everybody, we remark the entire revolution which has taken place upon the corners of Broadway since the "leg drama" made its appearance among us in the profusion it has within the past three years. Previously, nearly every corner of Broadway during the portions of the day when women most frequent it, would contain a group of "exquisites," whose lasci- vious eyes were eagerly searching about for the most exposed bosoms of the most beautiful ladies (?), or for the greatest exposure resulting from entering and leaving omnibuses. So common was this practice, that it became known to every woman that, wherever she might be upon the street, eager eyes were gazing upon her, ready to make the most of any situation she might be placed in. These institutions have nearly, if not quite, disappeared under the influence of the aforesaid drama, which by its very extravagance of exposure, has so far outstretched the street method that satiety has resulted. This is but another illustration of the fact that where little excites, profusion satisfies ; and people—men and women—now go and witness all the displays which it is possible to make of female beauty of form at our " Black Crooks" and " Les Brigands" and never think of becoming, vulgarly speaking, demoralized.

The application of this illustration is apparent. Children, by the little things they so readily gather about the difference of sex, are made curious to just the extent the means of satisfying that curiosity is difficult, and they pursue their means by stealth whenever and wherever possible. This results in producing a morbid condition of the mind about it, and encourages all kinds of secret vices, which are sapping the very life and beauty of the coming generation. No one can doubt this, who will give it the attention it merits, to be one of the crying ills of present systems of education. If instruction were begun in these matters at or about the age when curiosity is developed, and it is made a common matter of course, is it not plain that it would at once produce as effectual results as the case cited above ?

We are aware that "conservatives" will decry this plain way of treating this subject, and make use of the usual method of manifesting their condemnation ; nevertheless, the proposition to us is a simple one, over which we have spent many weary hours in the ineffectual endeavor to invest it with the drapery which society has veiled it by. A secret attracts everybody's attention. When it is a secret no longer it ceases to attract attention, and becomes reduced to its legitimate and natural uses. Without any hesitation, we assert our belief that the same results would follow the education of our children in sexual matters ; knowledge would succeed curiosity, and healthy action of the mind to a morbid desire. Think well before entering up a verdict of condemnation, for it is a point of vital import to humanity as a whole, as well as to individuals.

No. VII.

We now approach a part of the subject which is of supreme moment and that is the care which embryotic life demands in order that the required character shall be given the new organization, which having been the result of a union of two, brought about under the strictest application of adaptation, and of complete knowledge, begins its individualized existence. During this period of life, every influence to which the mother is subjected, be it ill or good, produces its legitimate effect upon the embryo. Whoever is an adept in these matters can go through society and from each individual tell what circumstances his or her mother was surrounded by during her pregnancy. To call to mind the truth of this we have but to refer to the "marking of children :" every other characteristic is equally the subject of the mother's surroundings. So it must become clear to every mother how terribly important this period of life is, and what a momentous responsibility she assumes when she undertakes the duties of an artist for humanity. And should such duties be entered upon thoughtlessly, carelessly, and with no regard whatever for them in a special sense ? Should marriages be consummated and these considerations be left out of the question, and never thought of until the actual responsibility is assumed ? Mothers of humanity ! yours is a fearful duty, and one which should in its importance lift you entirely above the modern customs of society, its frivolities, superficialities and deformities, and make you realize that to you is committed the divine work of perfecting humanity.

In this sense, and under this consideration, marriage becomes a thousand times more sacred than you or any other has ever regarded it. So fearfully sacred should it be that it should never be consummated until the researches of science and the teaching of wisdom are exhausted in the effort to prove that it will be a benefit to humanity.

It is because of this sacredness with which we regard the union of the sexes that we denounce the present marriage systems. Under these the interests of children are utterly ignored, and only the continuation of the union thought of, people all the while being deceived with the idea that it is for the children's sake that unfortunate unions should continue. No matter how illy-mated people may be, children will result. It will be difficult to find a case where an actual hate exists and not find children. What can be expected from children generated, born and raised under such influences ? There are numerous instances constantly being made public where mothers are even brutally treated during pregnancy, and oftentimes because they are pregnant. That such things are, is a standing impeachment against the rules of society, and a damning shame upon those, who would perpetuate them, under any circumstances.

Just the life the mother leads will she prepare her child to lead. Just what the mother desires to make her child she can mould and fashion it to be. What a comdemnation these considerations are upon the practices of fashionable society. How utterly worthless are the lives of so many mothers, and how devoid of purpose. Just so are their children. In the insane desire for dress and display, which characterizes so many women, lies the bane of life for their children. The cold heartlessness of the woman of fashion contains the germ of destruction for her daughter and the seeds of vice for her son. No warm-hearted, generous-souled children can spring from such soil. It can alone sow to the wind and reap the whirlwind.

Nor should the listless and unoccupied condition so many women fall into during pregnancy be much less discountenanced. Energy, purpose and application should be the very first considerations, and in just those directions it is desired the child should excel. In this respect, a thousand times more, are women the artists of humanity than they have ever thought. I remember once to have heard Mrs. Mary F. Davis deliver a lecture on "Woman as an Artist." Although quite young at that time it made a lasting impression upon me. It should be repeated in the hearing of every woman living until she should appreciate the full weight of the responsibility which the Creator has imposed upon her.

The practice of abortion is one which spreads damnation world-wide. Not so much in those cases where it is accomplished, but in those much more numerous cases where it is desired, attempted, but not reached. As soon as a woman becomes conscious that she is pregnant and a desire comes up in her heart to shirk the duties it involves, that moment the fœtal life is the unloved, the unwished child. Is it to be wondered that there are so many undutiful children; so many who instinctively feel that they are "incumbrances" rather than the beautiful necessities of the home? Their curses blast the lives of thousands who should have been a blessing to themselves and the world.

Another practice prevails which can but be most disastrous to the child. When a woman finds herself pregnant she begins to hide herself from the world, for fear that it shall also know it. If the child live to birth the world must know it. Why should it be deemed so terribly immodest previously as to warrant the virtual confinement of the mother ?   What true mother's heart but bounds with pride and joy when she sees the beauteous results of her constructive work ?   Why should she not also feel a like happiness when she realizes she is performing that constructive process ?   Is it to be wondered that there are so many children lacking all confidence in themselves and so foolishly diffident that it follows them through life ?   It should be the pride of every wo- man to be the willing, the anxious, the contented mother, and if she be so under the guidance of the knowledge we deem essential she will never have cause to regret that she fulfilled the duties of maternity.   All of these practices which do so much to degenerate the character of chil- dren should be discountenanced by every humanitarian, and every wo- man encouraged and assisted to wisely and perfectly mould and fashion the life which they shall give to the world.

We should feel satisfied with having performed sufficient for one life if we could bring humanity to regard these matters sufficiently to make them feel the necessity of reform in the entire circumstances which attend the bearing of children as deeply as we feel it.   We are con- vinced that this is the point to which effort must be directed, that hu- manity may be relieved of the continued production of the veriest abor- tions of manhood and womanhood in human shapes, by which it is now so extensively cursed.   Child-bearing must be made an aim in marriage, and no longer left to be its merest chance.   Children have a right to be born according to the very best methods which science can lay down, and men and women have no right to disregard this right, least of all to trample upon it.

VIII

It will not be seriously questioned that children at birth are already possessed of the germs which shall develop as they increase in age, but which cannot, except by the most persistent efforts, understandingly di- rected, be radically changed.   The trite saying that " he was a born thief, murderer or fool," is accepted, and generally believed, but it does not seem to be realized of what moment it is or of what comprehensive- ness.   If it apply to the thief, the murderer and the idiot, it equally ap- plies to all modifications of these traits up to being entirely good ; so that every living person was born what he is, in fundamental traits of character, which in expression, are of course modified according to the surrounding influences which promote his growth.

But we must pass from ante-natal life to that which has so generally been considered the beginning of it, and here a searching examination develops little more to be aproved than found previously. Certain it is, however, that there is a limited time in which the mother's care natu- rally belongs to the child. Some have attempted to make it appear that the child should not continue dependent upon the mother for nourishment ; it is a sufficient answer to this that nature has provided that it should be so dependent, and except objectionable upon special grounds it should so be. How little scientific or acquired knowledge there is regarding the early care of children their immense death-rate clearly shows. It seems one of the most sorrowful things of life to see the merest babes drop off by the thousands, as they do, for the very true reason that the mothers do not know how to rear them. This is the only reason for their great mortality, and there are very many reasons why some definite action should be taken to stop this disgraceful fact.

If wives will become mothers without the knowledge requisite to fit them to perform their duties to their children, then they should themselves be put under the care of some competent authority, so that the life they have been instrumental in organizing may not be uselssly thrown away. Every child properly conceived and born should live to be reared. Their should be a less proportionate mortality among them than among adults, because they are not necessarily subject to so many contingencies and exigencies which precipitate fatal consequences as they are. Everything which is required to insure the life of a healthy born child is proper care, natural diet, and judicious exercise, and no woman is fit to become a mother unless she know what all these are. If these are not reasonable conclusions then none can be deduced from the premises ; but, on the contrary, it must be concluded that it is just and right that children should be left to come into natural existence by chance ; that no primary considerations should be entertained regarding their production. But the time does come in which their demands are taken up, in which it is acknowledged that they have rights which must be respected, and powers and inherent ca- pacities which must be cared for and directed. When do these de- mands arise ? At what particular age do these come to be of signifi- cance ? There can be but one answer to this, and that is in direct op- position to, and refutation of, all present practice—at the very moment of the beginning of existence.

We are arguing, are pleading, are urging the rights of children ; those rights which shall make every child, male and female, honorable and useful members of society ; when they shall be considered as individual determining parts of it. Whether in acquiring this right all old forms, all present customs, all supposed interests are found to be standing in the way, matters not, the question is and must be recognized to be, What is for the best interests of children, not merely as children, but principally as the basis of future society ? Scarcely any of the practices of education, of family duties or of society's rights in regard to children are worthy of anything but the severest condemnation. They do not have their inherent rights at all in view. They consult the affections to the exclusion of all reason and common sense. They forget that the human is more than an affectional being ; that he has other than family duties to fulfill, and that he belongs to humanity, which is utterly ignored by all present practices.

Let the father and mother of every family ask themselves : Are we fully capable of so rearing our children that no other means could make them better citizens, and better men and women ? And how many could conscientiously give you an affirmative answer ? The fact that children are born and grown to be citizens, and not to remain children of the parents simply, is over-looked.

It is a matter worthy of the most serious and immediate consideration, whether the future good of children and society shall be sacrificed to the mere affectional relations of parents and children. No sensible person can look around among his or her circle of acquaintances and not become convinced that in certain cases children would be better off were they entirely withdrawn from the care of their parents.

We are aware that this, if intended for any considerable and comprehensive application, would be regarded as a startling assertion. Many true things when first announced startle the world, which thought differently so long. For ourselves we make the distinct asseveration that we are thoroughly convinced that fully one-half the whole number of children now living between the ages of ten and fifteen would have been in a superior condition, physically, mentally and morally to what they are, had they been early intrusted to the care of the proper kind of industrial institutions. It is useless to attempt to ignore the fact that home influences are not always the most beneficial to children. It is a well-known fact that these influences are absolutely detrimental in many instances. If this is so, to even the extent, that every one who will give it a moment's consideration must acknowledge it to be, does it not demand attention ?

We hold it to be an absolute and a fundamental right that every child, female and male, has, that when they are received into society, as determining powers, they shall be possessed of the required capacity and experience to take care of themselves, and to perform whatever may be required of them. We also lay it down as an absolute truth, —and no one will question it—that those who are best prepared to fulfill all the duties which can by any possibility devolve upon them as members of society, are the best citizens, and give unanswerable evidence of having been the recipients of the best means of growth and education.

To make the best citizens of children, then, is the object of education, and in whatever way this can be best attained, that is the one which should be pursued, even if it be to the complete abrogation of the present supposed rights of parents to control them. It is better that parents should be able to look with pride upon their children grown into maturity, as useful citizens by the assistance of the State, having been unable to make them thus themselves, than to consult the present sentiments of the heart, by having them constantly under their care and by so doing allow them to grow into maturity in form and grace, yet lacking the necessary elements developed in practice to make them acceptable to, or to be desired by, society. One of these would be the result of the existence of wisdom of affection, guided by reason ; the other that of selfishness, in which the good of the child would be sunk in the mere promptings of affection, regardless of consequences. No reasonable person can question which of the two is the better for all concerned, for children, for patents and for society.

The weight of our proposition, that society is itself responsible to children for the condition in which they are admitted to it as constituent members of itself, must begin to be apparent, for so far as they are concerned up to that time they are not responsible. This being self-evident, is it not also self-evident that they cannot with any consideration of justice be held to account for that which is the legitimate consequences of, and which is positively determined by, that condition?

We trust the time is near when the rights and privileges of children will be duly accorded and guaranteed to them by society, and when their true relations to society will be scientifically analyzed and understood and properly enforced.

www.ingramcontent.com/pod-product-compliance
Lightning Source LLC
Chambersburg PA
CBHW030554270326
41927CB00007B/910